Walking with Love and Autism

Walking with Love and Autism

Jo Austin

ATHENA PRESS
LONDON

WALKING WITH LOVE AND AUTISM
Copyright © Jo Austin 2010

All Rights Reserved

No part of this book may be reproduced in any form
by photocopying or by any electronic or mechanical means,
including information storage or retrieval systems,
without permission in writing from both the copyright
owner and the publisher of this book.

ISBN 978 1 84748 714 8

First published 2010 by
ATHENA PRESS
Queen's House, 2 Holly Road
Twickenham TW1 4EG
United Kingdom

Every effort has been made to trace the copyright holders
of works quoted within this book and obtain permissions.
The publisher apologises for any omission and will be happy to
make necessary changes in subsequent print runs.

Printed for Athena Press

With all my love, Robert,
I devote this book to you,
And youngsters like you
Everywhere.
Love you, Robert!
Love Mum!

A Love Poem

My mum love me so much
That my mum gives me a warm home
And my mum keeps me every day
And that's why my mum love me!

                                        by Jennifer, aged six

Acknowledgements

Where can one start when trying to thank so many people? I will try not to forget anyone, so here goes.

Thanks generally to everyone I know, as not one person laughed when I said I was going to write a book! Now, thanks to everyone's encouragement, I am writing book number three.

Thank you, most importantly, to my three wonderful children for just being children; I love you with all my heart.

Thank you to my sister Jan, who was the first person to read any of my writing and who is my best friend in the whole world. She's always been with me and the children, loving and supporting us every step of the way – I thank you and love you, Jan.

A special thank you must go to my dad for just being himself and remaining close to me and my children.

Thanks to my niece and my nephews, who have been greatly accepting, loyal, supportive and encouraging of Robert and the entire family, particularly during difficult times.

For the four people who helped me put all this together by typing my manuscript, which cannot have been easy as my writing was difficult and the subject emotional, a very big *THANK YOU* to my mum, my grandmother, Cecilia Windebank and especially to my youngest daughter Catherine, who finished it all off.

When God invented health visitors he must have had mine in mind. Thank you, Debbie Clutterbuck, Alison Choulerton and Alison Lewis-Smith.

To Anne, my best friend, who has stood by me for the past eight years. In good times and in bad, she has always been there for me. I need to thank you, Anne, for even standing by me when I've made mistakes and most of all for all those best-friend good bits!

To my children's schools and their staff for providing such wonderful, caring places for my children to learn and grow in, I thank you for your support. The schools I must mention include:

St Anthony's Catholic Primary School in Locksheath.

Heathfield Special School in Fareham.

St Peter's Catholic Primary School in Waterlooville.

Oaklands Catholic Secondary School and Sixth Form College in Waterlooville.

South Downs College Catering Department and Special Needs Support Team in Waterlooville.

To Hampshire Autistic Society, who have helped me, especially in these last two years. Special thanks for the support from Barbara and Carol.

Father Kevin Bidgood, our parish priest, must have a very special thank you: firstly as he is the person who gave the book its name, and secondly, he deserves our most sincere gratitude for his attention, guidance and support during the last few years, especially throughout a most difficult time for me personally.

To the whole parish of the Sacred Heart Church in Waterlooville, I must thank everyone in this most wonderful parish for their encouragement and support during the writing of this book and for their prayers throughout my time of ill health. We have a beautiful parish and that's the people, not just the building, and I have made many friends here, old and new.

To Martin Lewis, my thanks for providing the photo for the front cover of this book.

My list of acknowledgements would not be complete if I did not mention Father Chris Jordan, a family friend; my Auntie Chrissie, who is a great friend and confidante who gives me great strength; Rosemary, a very dear cousin; and all my family and friends.

I thank you and love you all!

Foreword

I am writing this book for despairing parents everywhere. Those who have been blessed with a 'special' child will know the heartache, the joys and the frustrations I hope to share with you by writing this. I do not offer advice or solutions – who am I to offer these? I can only share understanding, sympathy and hope, and a light-hearted look at life, real life experienced by real people with real problems.

Mainly, I hope that by sharing my thoughts and experiences I can offer comfort to all those parents with children who have special needs.

I wish I could say to parents, 'Do not despair', as I know we all do despair at times. What I can say is that you are not alone but that there are times when we are all low, and again there are times when we thank God for our children because, for whatever reason, we have been blessed; in God's wondrous way, he has given us such special, loving children and all he asks in return is that we love them. Love is all they need and love is certainly what we can all give them.

Contents

This is Life	13
Our Baby Boy	15
That First Year	18
What a Silent World	23
Talk to Me!	29
A Word about Discipline	31
And Then There Were Three	37
Is Anybody Listening?	42
Help!	54
Stop Trying to Be Perfect	67
The Parent and Child Game	73
Destination Diagnosis	75
A New Beginning	78
No More Drugs	81
Meeting Dan	83
The Transition to Oaklands	85
The Beginning of the Depression	89
Turnaround	92
Robert's Greatest Day	94
Epilogue – Robert's Miracle	97

This is Life

A wonderful lady once told me that 'life is to be enjoyed, not endured'. I will never forget these words as they have often proved invaluable when, during times of stress, they have somehow popped into my mind and reminded me that life is good and that we are all very lucky indeed to be alive. We really should make the very best of life and enjoy it to the full.

This is not to say that I don't get down; sure I do. I have good days and bad days just like everyone else, but somehow past experiences seem to return to remind me that you can do something to improve things. We all have the power within us to change, hopefully for the better. I would like to think that all my past experiences, whether good or bad, have helped to make me a better person, and allowed me to live and learn. That's what life is all about.

Many times over the past years I have despaired, when my husband and I have both been low and exhausted. We have also been at our wits' end, not knowing where to turn, what to do next. However, we have also had to learn to accept that nobody has all the answers right now, that we must just be patient and just wait and see. In the meantime, we have accepted that this is life. This is our life, and if we want to enjoy it and enable our children to enjoy life to the full, then we must get on with it and make the very best out of it.

Life is good, and I remain determined that my family will have a good life and just simply enjoy themselves, and grow up to be responsible adults. I ask no more than to be able to raise my children, with or without special needs, to be decent, kind, loving Christian people who in turn will be able to radiate joy and laughter to all with whom they come into contact.

I think here would be a good point to mention that I am by no means a perfect mother. I sometimes shout and make mistakes with the children and my husband. Indeed, I expect I've made

This is Life

many mistakes, especially in the manner in which I've tried to bring up my children. However, none of us is trained in the very difficult task of being a parent; each of us has to do what we believe is best for our children. I would say that being a mother is the most demanding role I have ever undertaken, and I have done many other taxing jobs in the past. But it is also the most rewarding, and I certainly wouldn't swap my life for the world.

All I can say is that no matter what we do for our children, whether right or wrong, we do so with the very best of our intentions. I just hope that most of the time we get it right, and whatever happens at the end of the day, I know that I love my children and they know I love them. My children are safe, loved and loving, and that is what matters the most.

Our Baby Boy

I don't imagine there is one mother or father who cannot remember the midwife's words upon delivery of their beautiful precious child. The words, 'It's a girl' or 'It's a boy' have to be the most wonderful words one ever utters to another human being. Certainly in our case this was very true.

We will never forget those magical moments, the births of all of our children. Each was wonderful and precious. What a great gift to be presented with such perfect, tiny miracles! However, I have to be honest and say that each time I hoped the midwife would say, 'It's a girl.' Presumably this stems from the fact that in our family we only ever seem to favour girls; certainly on my maternal side, we gave birth mainly to females.

Needless to say, all my family were delighted with the news of my second pregnancy, and having one daughter already, the usual response was, 'Let's hope for a boy this time.' I have to admit, secretly I still hoped for another girl. I was only used to girls and had only ever dealt with baby girls. The thought of having two girls of my own was wonderful. I had no idea what little boys were like and am now totally ashamed to think that I would really rather not have had one, thank you very much.

However, God saw fit to present me with a baby boy and I thank God for ignoring my prayers for another girl (yes, I really did pray for a girl!) so there we were in the delivery room and the midwife said those amazing words, 'It's a boy.' My immediate thoughts were not quite as negative as I would have expected. I actually remember thinking, He's born, he's alive, he's healthy and he's mine. It didn't really matter what sex he was, although my very next thought was how on earth was I going to react to a baby boy? I needn't have given it another thought, though, because the very next moment my baby boy was in my arms and I fell in love with him. Such immediate, total, unconditional love was indeed an overwhelming feeling.

Our Baby Boy

I don't know who was more surprised about the birth of our baby boy, me or my family, because, although they had all hoped it would be a boy, they had assumed, as I had done, that it would be another girl. After all, our family only had girls, didn't it?

I must just add at this point that, since that wondrous moment, my sister has also been blessed with a baby boy, after a girl as her firstborn. Thank you, God, for allowing her to share with me the joy of having children of both sexes. What a wonderful life experience!

Having revelled in my baby boy, it's not to say I love my girls any less. Now I am happy to say that I love girls and I love boys. They may certainly be slightly different ways of loving, but the love is divided equally between my children.

I hope that it is true to say now that most parents, no matter what their previous preferences are to the sex of their babies, actually find that you quite simply love what you are given. We have no choice in this matter; nature or God, whatever you believe in, seems to settle this matter for the best.

So if there is anyone out there expecting a baby soon and hoping, maybe even praying, for one sex or the other, all I can say is even if you don't get your wish, I'm sure you won't be disappointed.

Our baby boy soon became the apple of everybody's eyes. He in turn rewarded us a thousand times over with an abundance of love and affection, this being attributed to his being a little boy. His cup was indeed overflowing.

Shortly after the birth of our son, a friend of mine sent me a copy of a poem she had kept for many years, given to her after the birth of her sons. She now has three! She was always aware of my desire for two girls, and could not understand my reasoning. I can now, of course, say to her quite honestly that I am more than happy to have children of both sexes. However, I have also come to realise that to have children all of one gender is equally fulfilling, and I would still be just as content. I am sure that all parents love their children irrespective of gender and would be devastated to hear anyone say of either all girls or all boys, 'Poor you!'

The gender of our offspring is obviously something we cannot control, so before sympathising with parents of children of just one gender, or of both, I think we must all remember that we all love our children no matter what and are thankful for them whatever their gender. After all, I am sure that most mums and dads agree, any child is a blessing.

I can now say that I have no preference for girls or boys, but I will leave this chapter with the poem sent by my friend. I had never been able to understand why she raved about her boys. How naive of me.

What Is a Boy?

He's an imp and an angel, a dreamer, a tease,
An explorer of meadows and a climber of trees;
A runner of errands, a doer of chores,
Who tears his best trousers, and tracks up your floors.
He's a solemn young man with some mud on his
    feet,
And a daredevil riding his bike down the street;
A bundle of questions who wants to know why
The world goes around and the stars fill the sky.
But adventurous, timid, excited or quiet,
There's nothing so new that he won't care to try it,
And just when your patience and temper wear thin,
He'll look up at you with an innocent grin,
And your heart melts again with your real pride and
    joy,
In that mischievous, wonderful treasure – your boy!

Heather Short

That First Year

I cannot pretend that the first year with Robert was an easy one; far from it. However, having already had one child (Jennifer was, in fact, still only a baby herself) now twenty-one months old when Robert was born, and realising just how quickly they grow and change, I was determined I was going to enjoy his first year.

I decided, when I first knew I was pregnant again, that I would breastfeed this time. I didn't breastfeed the first time round, for many reasons. Deep down, I had always felt guilt and a pang of regret about this decision and had often wondered what it would be like and if it would have gone well for us. However, I was young and naive and in fact the thought of breastfeeding did not appeal to me at all when I had my first baby. I had convinced myself that if I wasn't really keen on breastfeeding then the tension and stress may be transmitted to the baby and it would not go well anyway, and then I would have to change to bottles and start all over again with something new.

We also happened to be moving house the very week that Jennifer was born, so for all these reasons at the time, rightly or wrongly, I chose to bottle-feed and thought I was doing the right thing. Jennifer in fact, turned out to be a wonderful baby, a real pleasure, a textbook baby. She fed regularly at three-hour intervals, she slept well during the day and night and was quite a bundle of fun.

To add to all this, I recovered quickly from the pregnancy and birth. I wasn't tired and I enjoyed my baby. We were, however, spoilt by all this as Jennifer slept through the night after just five weeks, reached all the milestones ahead of schedule and presented as an 'ideal baby'. Maybe some of this was just us trying too hard to get it all right and do it all by the book.

Soon though I began to feel I hadn't done it right at all, I hadn't given her my best; I felt I should at least have tried to breastfeed her.

That First Year

Thus armed with all this new information, regrets and guilt, together with an undying determination to get it all right second time around, I knew I was going to breastfeed Robert successfully because I felt so positive about it. I guess I also thought at least there was nothing else for me to learn, as I'd done the rest before.

This positive attitude and sheer determination won and did the trick; the breastfeeding was quickly and easily established. I found myself surprised to be saying that I actually enjoyed breastfeeding. What a shame I hadn't been more encouraged the first time round. It really was a pleasant feeling feeding my son!

I loved all the cuddling and the closeness we felt and the bonding was wonderful. The sheer dependence and intimacy of those moments was a marvel. I can't, however, paint a picture of total harmony and perfection here, though, as there were times when, after seemingly feeding the baby for hours on end and feeling totally and utterly exhausted, I would long for sleep, and when resting my head on the pillow, feeling that sleep was imminent, the baby would wake, crying to be fed again! I am sure many of us at these times have thought, I cannot feed you any more today! Please, just let me sleep a while.

I very quickly noticed this amazing difference between breastfeeding and bottle-feeding. I was exhausted!

Had Robert been our first baby, this maybe wouldn't have been noticed so much, as I could have rested more when he slept, but having one very energetic, enthusiastic and extremely inquisitive toddler to look after as well really did add up to double trouble.

Although the feeling of breastfeeding was wonderful, Robert never seemed to settle much past the initial two hours. Again, in hindsight, perhaps I shouldn't have given in so much to him. Maybe he really didn't need feeding all those times, but Robert seemed to be an extremely sensitive, restless baby. Looking back now, it's easy to see why, but at the time, in our ignorance, we just did our best.

Robert only ever seemed to respond to the stimulus of being held, touched, cuddled, and above all nursed at the breast. Luckily, having decided that I was going to enjoy his first year, I relaxed a bit more than with the first baby. I let the house go a little bit more and devoted myself to trying to be a good mummy and giving him as much attention as he wanted in the early months. Some may say I was guilty of overindulging and spoiling him, but luckily, as it turns out, he really did need this, and thankfully, I now have no regrets about the attention I gave him.

I feel that I gave him my best when he needed me most and it also helped me to realise that it didn't matter that I hadn't breastfed Jennifer, because she too had her share of attention, cuddles and love as a baby. I realised that at the time I did what I felt was right for her and that she too had our devotion, but in a slightly different way. In fact, she had the devotion of the entire family as Daddy and Gran also enjoyed feeding her and holding her close as a tiny baby. They too had shared in that feeling of dependence and devotion.

So I have come to realise there is good and bad in most things, as there is in most people, and as my own sister is very good at doing, I am learning to find good in everything and everybody!

As I was saying, Robert seemed to be quite a demanding baby and after four months I gave up breastfeeding him, hoping that I might feel less exhausted and that he for once might settle better and we might even get a good night's sleep. There had been no physical problems with the breastfeeding, such as mastitis, sore or cracked nipples, engorgement or anything. I felt it had all come quite naturally. I had a good milk supply, Robert latched on beautifully and we were both enjoying it. So I felt a little disappointed giving up, and found it a difficult decision to make. I remember thinking at the time, I love having babies, I love breastfeeding; I hope I can have another baby because I want to do this all again.

Bottle-feeding didn't go quite as I expected, either. But again, we were unaware at the time that Robert had any problems. We found out at ten months that his tonsils and adenoids were huge, but at the time of changing from breast to bottle I became very frustrated that feeding time, which was supposed to be a pleasant experience, was turning into something to dread.

I had assumed that Robert would have a good feed and settle really contentedly after the formula milk, and I had imagined we would still be close and loving at feed time. Instead, Robert would

That First Year

cough and splutter and one or other of us, usually both, would end up wearing most of the feed!

Robert still didn't sleep through the night and still didn't settle too well but I convinced myself it would get better. I actually put most of Robert's behaviour down to the fact that he was a boy and that he was a second child. I had been told often that boys are slower than girls and that the second child doesn't always reach milestones as quickly as their sibling. So I quite naively thought he was just a lazy, sensitive boy.

I must admit, I didn't watch for every milestone and achievement quite in the same way as I had with Jennifer, but again I thought I shouldn't expect him to be as advanced as she was. Who, these days, has time to watch out for all these things when one has two young children, living as we do at such a pace in today's stressful society?

Imagine our surprise, therefore, when at eight months old, Robert had his development test and failed to respond to any of the sounds used for the hearing checks! I remember the health visitor saying, 'Never mind, he has probably got a cold. We'll check again in a few weeks' time when he is feeling better.'

A few weeks later, when we returned for the hearing checks, Robert seemed quite well but again he failed to respond to any of the sounds. I don't really know who was more surprised, the health visitor or me. We looked at each other with total surprise and disbelief. I felt quite shocked as she said she would refer him to the clinic for a full hearing test.

Shortly after this, Robert had a chest infection, one of many in his first year. This time, he seemed bluer than usual around the lips and was really struggling for breath. I called the doctor and he was rushed into hospital with upper-airways obstruction. This was partly due to the fact that he had a chest infection but also due to his having very large tonsils and adenoids, which really did not help the problem.

We had guessed by this time that Robert's tonsils and adenoids would have to be removed at some point, but we had not appreciated the effect this was having on his hearing. Robert was monitored overnight while in hospital, given Ventolin nebulisers and we left the following day without realising that Robert was also seriously asthmatic.

That First Year

The appointment for Robert's hearing test came through quite quickly, much to our relief, but again Robert performed quite poorly. Although not totally deaf, he had very little hearing. My husband Mike and I still had not put two and two together and realised the connection with the tonsils. How very pathetic of me, you might say, as I had in fact trained as a nurse myself and worked many times in the ear, nose and throat wards!

I can assure you, though, that no amount of training in child care, nursing or raising children prepares you for your own offspring. Far from it. In fact, sometimes I think a little knowledge can do more harm than good. We imagined all sorts of things could be wrong with our son, emotions took over and common sense didn't stand a chance.

What a Silent World

After the hearing test, I remember the audiologist saying he would refer Robert to the ear, nose and throat specialist. He told us the appointment would be sent through the post and sent us off home, telling us to be patient.

I went to my mum's that afternoon and broke down, yet again, (there had been many instances of tears with my mum). I remember saying, 'What if he never hears me say "I love you"!'

It seemed like an eternity until he saw the ENT consultant, but we were lucky as he was actually seen two weeks later in an emergency clinic. The consultant, as we expected, said she would have to remove Robert's tonsils and adenoids and at the same time would put grommets in his ears. The penny dropped and suddenly I felt quite stupid that I hadn't realised of course that his hearing would improve once his tonsils and adenoids were out of the way and his ears were drained with the grommets.

The consultant said she would perform surgery as soon as Robert was fit enough for operation, as they really were making his life a misery; he was still having difficulty feeding and breathing. We went away feeling quite high. Our emotions had been up and down like yo-yos for some time. We thought that the end was in sight and that any day now Robert would have his op and all would be well.

Robert wasn't going to let us off the hook that easily. He then had infection after infection and it seemed he was never going to be fit enough for surgery. A time did come, however, when for all intents and purposes he seemed quite fit and well. We were given a date two weeks later and prepared ourselves for D-Day.

Of course, looking back now, it all makes sense why Robert was so restless as a baby, why he only responded to cuddling, touching and nursing frequently. He didn't respond to the sound of voices and I didn't even notice. How ashamed I feel that I missed this. How surprised we were when he failed his eight-month hearing check. Everyone tried to reassure me that you don't notice so much with your second baby and I really did think that he was just a typical boy, a little lazy perhaps, or a bit slower than his sister and extremely loving and sensitive. But I am his mummy and I feel I should have noticed these things. It's just a good job I did give in to his demands to be loved and cuddled all the time. I have no regrets on that. He needed me and luckily I responded as naturally as I believed I could.

So we made arrangements for the operation day. We arranged for Jennifer to stay with her gran for a few days, Mike took some time off work and I prepared overnight bags for Robert and myself. We had been advised to allow two days in hospital: the day of the op and the following day to check all was well. I had images already of this perfectly healthy, happy, hearing baby boy that I would bring home, although at the same time I was of course very emotional about my baby having an operation and anaesthetic.

From the moment I left him in the anaesthetic room, he was no longer totally dependent on me. In a way, we had to hand over our baby to the doctors and trust in them completely, something I found very hard to come to terms with. I cried as I walked away from him asleep in that room. He looked so small and vulnerable and I just wanted to run away with him. But I knew deep down he needed the operation to improve his quality of life, so who was I to deny him that? Our emotions again were rising and falling like yo-yos!

The anaesthetist was not completely convinced that Robert was fit enough but like us thought we would never catch him in a much better condition. So he agreed to proceed with the operation. Having seen many doctors in the last year, with Robert's repeated chest infections and feeding problems, I was amazed that this was the first doctor who really agreed with me that there was something not quite right about Robert, but he couldn't put his finger on it. I think he felt a little dubious or uneasy about the whole thing.

So, mums, what I am saying here is stand by your instincts; Mum really does know best! I had been saying for a long time that Robert was much more poorly than anyone else was prepared to

What a Silent World

believe. I even convinced myself that I was being a little neurotic, as I'm sure that was what most doctors were thinking. I began to play things down a little too, and I reassured myself that soon it would all be over. All these thoughts were going through my mind as I waited for the time to pass, as the nurse had said, 'He'll be back on the ward in just forty minutes,' and that would be the end of all these problems.

Forty minutes came and went; in fact, an hour came and went. Other children were returning from their operations but there was still no sign of my Robert. I looked at Mike, who in turn was looking at his watch again and looking very worried. I didn't speak to him as I struggled to resist the silent panic rising inside me. I kept telling myself everything was OK, and he would be back in a minute.

A nurse popped her head round the door and disappeared again. I heard her in the corridor outside as she said, 'Yes, they are in here – shall I call them?' She returned to the room and said, 'Don't panic, but the doctor would like to see you in the operating suite.'

I remember thinking what a funny thing to say; of course we were panicking. Why couldn't she just tell us what was wrong? Of course, she couldn't tell us because she didn't know; she just knew there was a problem and had been told to fetch us.

I couldn't accept this. I thought that she couldn't tell us because he was dead and wanted the doctor to tell us. How silly of me. Did I honestly think the doctor would make us walk down that long, long corridor to the operating suite, fearing the worst? She obviously didn't realise the tricks one's mind plays during times of such stress. Of course if he had been dead the doctor would have come to us.

I was so relieved to find that my baby was alive but I still couldn't stop crying. I had cried all the way down that long, long corridor. (I had walked down that corridor so many times as a nurse but as a mummy it was the longest walk I'd ever done in the world.) I was shaking now and felt I was losing control. I told myself to get a grip, sort myself out and get some composure; we needed to understand what the doctors were telling us.

The doctor explained that Robert had had an asthma attack

under the anaesthetic and that his right lung had collapsed. She said that they were ventilating him and that he was being taken to intensive care as he would require artificial ventilation for a while yet. As I started to cry again, she became the firm but gentle doctor I remembered her to be from working with her some years earlier. She reminded me that I really did know this was for the best and that they would have everything under control. She also reminded me that they would always be totally honest with us.

It was going to be some time apparently before they would be ready for Robert in intensive care, and under normal circumstances it would have been some time before we could see him. However, the doctor thankfully very quickly realised that I would be much more reassured if I could see Robert immediately. She was right. Robert had to remain in the operating suite to be ventilated until intensive care were ready for him. There were other children waiting by now for their operations, which had to be done a little later than planned that day or postponed. I hope those patients can understand that the hospitals really do just do their best!

The doctor led me into the operating theatre. Robert's little body lay on what appeared at the time to be a hideously large bed for this tiny baby (the operating table). He was so still and looked so pale, and there were tubes everywhere. I should have been more prepared for this, but again, when it's your own child lying there, emotions play havoc with you and certainly don't give your brain a chance.

Robert looked so alone and vulnerable and I felt so helpless. I couldn't pick him up and run away with him, which is what I wanted to do, so I kissed him and whispered, 'Mummy loves you, see you in a bit.' I did at least by now feel more reassured that he was alive, and where there's life there's hope!

We sat in the lounge outside intensive care as they settled Robert in and prepared for us to see him. Mike phoned the family to explain what had happened and the nurse phoned for the hospital chaplain to come and sit with us as we had requested. The chaplain happened to be a family friend and had officiated at our marriage. Thankfully, his new job was that of hospital chaplain so he sat with us frequently over the next few horrific days; he even made the tea for us when Jennifer came to visit with Gran. He tried hard to maintain some kind of normality for the whole family. He needn't have said a word in all that time; just his presence was reassuring and comforting. Having a friend like him around made me feel I had sort of a short cut to God. I kind of jumped the queue with him to get my prayers answered because I had this helping hand up the ladder, so to speak!

And goodness, did we pray! So many people prayed for Robert. My family, Mike's family, our church, Mike's mum's church, the chaplain and all sorts of other people who heard about him. God probably thought he had better sort this one out as he was getting earache.

It's strange to think I didn't ask God to make him better than he was before the operation, just to let him live. In fact, at that moment, when he was on the ventilator, I wasn't even sure if the operation was finished. I didn't even know how far in the operation they had gone before they ran into problems. I remember the doctor saying at least his tonsils were in the bin; they really did need to come out. I was not sure though if they had managed to get the grommets in and I really didn't care. I thought I would really rather have him not hearing than not have him at all. I vowed that he would never have another operation, unless it was a question of life or death. Maybe that's a bit selfish. I mean, would he thank me when he was a bit older if his hearing was not very good and was affecting his quality of life? Well, I didn't know. That was something to worry about if the problem arose, certainly not at that point.

I just thank God that he answered our prayers this time. Robert recovered and was taken off the ventilator after three days and remained in intensive care for a further twenty-four hours to make sure he could maintain his breathing on his own. I'm not sure where people get their strength from at times like these but Mike and I remained at his side while he was in intensive care and had very little sleep. We were given a little room near IC with a couple of camp beds in to get some rest but I just couldn't leave him. I remained by his side. I stayed at the hospital with Robert for a further three days on the ward while he recovered. He had frequent Ventolin nebulisers and antibiotics, began to eat again and gradually improved in his general health.

Robert started to smile and laugh and amuse everyone again but he still slept little at night and I was exhausted! The family came in often to keep us company, take him for walks in his pram and generally try to give me a break. I finally left his side to go home to Mum's for a bath and a rest (and a decent meal). I stayed away for a full two hours before I felt compelled to return to his side.

The next day I went to the hospital church service, and an old man asked me if I had a relative in the hospital. I explained briefly and added that Robert was getting better now. He didn't say another word, he just put his hand on my shoulder as I cried once again. Thankfully, they were tears of relief and happiness. I remember there were mostly old people at the service with many in wheelchairs and I thought, what a shame if it takes us until old age to discover the wonders of God. It was a beautiful service, with all my favourite hymns, but I couldn't sing the words.

It was so very emotional. Lots of the old people were crying too, and I thought, We're lucky to be young and alive, with our young family. Alive!

I thanked God again and returned to my baby. They let us go home that afternoon!

Thank you, God, for my son, and thank you for my family.

Talk to Me!

Having written the previous chapter, I found it impossible to carry on writing for a while. I couldn't bring myself to read back over what I had written up to this point. So I put away the paper and decided it would be best to have a bit of a break for a while. It was, after all, quite emotional writing some of the chapters, and in particular the previous one. I also thought it was about time I shared my thoughts with some other people in order to determine whether or not to carry on with the book.

My sister was the first person to read what I had written. Obviously, having been brought up together and having the same parents, our thoughts and beliefs are quite similar. I did not, however, expect her to be in tears throughout the whole of the first chapters. When she had finished reading, we cuddled and we both cried. If nothing else, writing all this had been extremely therapeutic.

She said it was wonderful and certainly worth carrying on with. From her reaction, I was determined that I would finish the book and if it helped only one other parent to feel that there was hope, and that there were other people sharing and caring about the joys and heartaches of life with special children (in fact, any children), then it will have been worth it.

It's funny the things people say or don't say during times of stress. The things you try to forget. Yet amazingly, years later, despite thinking that you had pushed them right to the back of your mind, they come flooding back, as clear as if they had happened yesterday. I certainly find I can remember many things in precise detail that I had thought I would not be able to recall.

My sister said she had no idea what we'd been through. This is when we first started to talk about what had happened and shared our memories and feelings of the time when Robert was on the ventilator. I hadn't really talked about it like this with anybody; we really had just not talked about it. Strange how we

Talk to Me!

(people in general) don't seem to talk about things that hurt. And yet what powerful healers, talking, listening, and sharing are! They really make quite a difference.

There were things Jan (my sister) said later that made me realise that she had gone through it too. She said when she first came into intensive care to see us and she saw Robert attached to all the tubes, all she kept thinking was that she mustn't cry because she didn't want to upset me any more. I, in turn, was thinking that this was all she needed, seeing her nephew like this when at the time she was three months' pregnant with her little son! Funny how you still find time to think of others. She squeezed my hand and we said nothing. Just being together is often all the comfort that is needed; words are not always necessary (though I must admit to being one of the world's most incessant chatterboxes). I find much solace in talking about (and writing about) everything and anything.

My sister added that she left intensive care and could contain the tears no longer as she waited for the lift. A lady asked her if she was all right. 'Not really,' she replied and explained the situation. The lady said she quite understood as she was a nurse! Jan should have said, 'So am I.' We both trained as nurses in the same hospital before taking time out to raise our own families.

I remember also at the time thinking how difficult it must have been for the nurse looking after Robert. She was with him for most of the time from the moment he first entered intensive care. I discovered after a day or so that at home she herself had a baby exactly the same age as Robert. How must she have felt looking after one so young, like her own and yet so poorly? She coped and responded very well indeed, if I remember rightly. She was extremely professional.

Later on, when Robert was recovering, she told me that she had struggled hard to fight back the tears when she let me in to see him for the first time on the ventilator. She said she found that quite difficult because obviously she could imagine exactly what I must be feeling. She was wonderful, that's all I can say, and I thank her for taking such good care of my son.

A Word about Discipline

Robert was eleven and a half months old when he had his operation. It was his first birthday, the week after he was allowed home. We had not really planned a party but after the ordeal we had all been through, we decided to celebrate. We invited everyone to share with us: family, friends, neighbours and all the children. It was wonderful.

My mum bought Robert a Noddy car, one of those pedal-along ones. She tied ribbons and balloons on it and we all watched in sheer delight as Robert was shown his new toy. I shall never forget the smile on his face that day. I don't think he stopped smiling all day and neither did we.

It seemed hard to believe now just how poorly he had been only a couple of weeks before. Robert's general health improved rapidly over the following year. He was diagnosed as asthmatic and we had to give him Ventolin inhalers with a mask over his face when he had an attack. These were quite frequent and frightening when he had just come home from hospital; he didn't like the mask but it made him better. The attacks lessened and he seemed to grow out of it, with attacks as infrequent as once a year eventually.

Along with his improved health, Robert started to talk; just one word at a time but definitely words. In fact, in the first few months we were so excited as he seemed to copy so many words so quickly. Then he came to a standstill again. We knew he should be progressing on to two words together and more but it didn't happen. People kept telling us to be patient but Robert was now beginning to get frustrated and we were feeling a little disappointed again.

We tried all the usual things: talking slowly and deliberately to him, and pronouncing each word really clearly, but he seemed to get even more frustrated. I think he knew there should be something more. I don't think we are stupid parents by any

A Word about Discipline

means; we really did try for Robert, but he just reverted to pointing at things and saying 'Ugh!' for what he wanted. We tried not giving him what he wanted, such as a drink, for example, unless he said the word and maybe even 'please', but it just seemed to make him worse. Robert started to have many tantrums and his behaviour seemed so erratic. There were really good periods when he seemed quite calm and tried really hard and then there would be times when he regressed and his behaviour would be quite unpredictable.

I must admit that when he first came home from hospital, I seemed to be somewhat lacking in my approach to discipline with both the children. I was so glad to have them that I found it very difficult to say no to either of them! Needless to say, eventually, with the children getting their own way all the time, things began to get out of control. Jennifer, especially, had been pretty well disciplined from the moment she was born, and is the type of child who needs very firm handling. She needs to know exactly where she stands, exactly what is or is not acceptable and just how far she can push you. In fact, I think this is fair to say of most children. They need to have very clear boundaries set and Jennifer is the type of child that, as I often say of her, 'If you give her an inch, she takes a mile!'

So we very quickly (well, after a month or so) realised that we were going to have to show more control and confidence in order to regain some degree of normality. I realised that we were spoiling the children, that to give in to their every whim did not in fact prove to them how much we loved them. Discipline is important for everyone. Indeed, we were not doing them any favours at all. I especially was guilty of gross overindulgence and of depriving my children of important knowledge and experience of what is right and wrong and of how to grow and learn with a healthy and moral attitude.

I once read a very good article about discipline that I will never forget. Luckily, I read the book at the time when we were beginning to reintroduce discipline into our home.

We started with the basics, getting back to normal mealtimes, not picking between meals, sitting at the table to eat and drink, not wandering around the house with food or drinks and getting

A Word about Discipline

back to normal bedtimes. These were all things we had been quite strict with before, but as I said, our discipline was somewhat lax for a while. Children need discipline and routine and I thought we had always been quite good at these, so I was surprised to find myself feeling guilty if I didn't give in to them. However, I read this article and it has always given me the strength to stick to my guns and be firm or gentle, but to discipline appropriately when I felt it was needed.

The article was really just a simple statement reinforcing the two faces of love. That love causes a person to act for the benefit of the loved one, and therefore it is love that gives the person the strength to act in the appropriate way, so that children learn from their parents' example that love may be a cuddle, a joy or a gentleness, or a reproach, reproof or punishment.

Children need to learn that love is spoken through the word 'no' as much as 'yes'. I am a firm believer in this teaching and that in fact not to discipline one's children is in truth proof of neglect rather than love. A child who grows up believing that love is only conveyed in moments of sweetness and gentleness, will not grow up a whole and happy person.

Having armed myself with a bit of reassuring common sense from a couple of helpful Mothercare books (*Toddler Taming* is a must for any young family) I began to feel much more confident in my approach to the children and felt that we were returning to a degree of normality.

The reintroduction of discipline and normality did wonders for Jennifer but sadly the same was not true for Robert.

Robert's behaviour seemed to deteriorate by the day. There were many tantrums and he seemed permanently frustrated. We put a lot of it down to the terrible twos and a lot to the fact that he had rather a traumatic first year.

We also took comfort in the fact that so many people kept telling us that he would soon catch up. 'He's just a bit behind,' they'd say, and add, 'he'll soon catch up!' We had to believe this to keep our own spirits high. We kept saying to ourselves that all of a sudden things would 'click' into place and Robert would start improving in leaps and bounds, especially in his speech and behaviour.

A Word about Discipline

'In a year or two, we'll look back and wonder what all the fuss was about. By then he will have caught up with his peers and all will be well.' This was another favourite saying, along with 'You must be more patient,' and 'Don't forget what he's been through,' as if we could ever forget!

And yet those same people offering these positive statements of reassurance (who were they trying to convince: us or themselves?) were the same people who did seem to forget so quickly what he'd been through. Another day would come statements like, 'Isn't he doing such and such yet? So and so down the road is!'

However, we were the ones living with Robert and beginning to realise daily that all was not as it should be.

While discipline was doing great things for Jennifer, we were beginning to find discipline totally disastrous for Robert. We really didn't know what to do for him. He was so frustrated and we again felt so helpless. He desperately needed routine and discipline yet he was so sensitive that discipline merely left him totally and utterly desperate, he was pitiful. He could not tolerate discipline from me in particular, and not from the rest of the family, either.

An utterance of the word 'no' or a cross tone would leave Robert screaming and thrashing. At best he would whimper in my arms for what seemed like hours. His behaviour became extremely negative and he was very difficult to direct. I wondered what had happened to my lovely little boy.

We took Robert for another hearing test. His hearing was fine, but he was referred for speech therapy and again we waited for the appointment for what seemed like an eternity. Again, we were pinning our hopes on yet another specialist.

As the speech therapist began the initial assessment, our spirits were lifted again as she reassured us that his behaviour was perfectly normal for a child with delayed speech and language comprehension and that as his speech improved so would his behaviour. We felt, once more, that there was light at the end of the tunnel and that things really would start to improve soon. She suggested that if he was still having problems when he was three, he might be able to attend a language group once a week with half

A Word about Discipline

a dozen children with similar problems. For the first time, it was actually I who thought he would be OK by then. She then offered us an appointment for three months hence and said he would be seen probably every three months. He was still not putting two words together and I suddenly felt shattered again. I wondered what good could possibly be done, as it averaged out at just four sessions a year.

We were doing all we could at home. I mean, we're quite a chatty family: we talk to our children, read books, play games and all the usual things that help with speech, without over-emphasising the problem too much. The last thing we wanted to do was pressure him. So we went home again and got on with life and got through the days the best we could.

I really have to admit here that I have never been the most patient person in the world but I hope that since having the children I have learnt more and more to try to be patient. Robert, in fact, seemed to need an abundance of patience and I found that the only way to get through the day with any amount of sanity left was simply to be so patient and calm with him that I merely found myself behaving differently from how I ever expected I would.

I tried turning a blind eye nine times out of ten and saved the discipline for when it was really important. This way, we could at least get through the day without too many battles.

When it really mattered, we could then use whatever measures were appropriate for discipline at difficult times, such as if he was going to hurt himself (or someone else), or if he was going to break something or run off out the door, for example. Some may say that I was certainly guilty of overindulgence but we were at least getting through the day with fewer battles and traumas than previously.

Many times I found that if my tone changed in the slightest, if my patience started swaying or my voice was raised even slightly, then we might just as well wipe out the rest of the day because I wouldn't be able to do a thing with him then. He simply could not cope! So we did what we could to get through each day!

Again, I had to remember that there is good in everybody and despite all this, there were still tender, loving moments when we

A Word about Discipline

simply cuddled for hours. What a wonderful way nature has of making these children so loving and loveable. Compensation is certainly given in the overwhelming love that is both given and received by these special children.

We had come to nickname Robert our Lovable Rogue. It was a saying that kept us going and brought some measure of reassurance that there is both good and bad in everybody. Sometimes you have to look a little harder but I am convinced that there is *always* some good. We had simply learnt to look at the good in Robert and enjoy it.

And Then There Were Three

The following year proved to be another hectic one. Robert's problems, however, seemed to have become a way of life and again we put it all down to the usual things like, 'He's a boy, he's our second child and he's had a very traumatic start to life!' We thought he would catch up or outgrow his present behaviour pattern and all would be well. So we got on with the day-to-day activities that everyone commonly associates with living.

Jennifer started playschool and Robert went to Gym-tots and Toddlers', while I battled hard against tantrums and offending stares. I tried to pretend it didn't bother me, as I tucked him under my arm and marched home after another awkward scene when Robert was told to do something (or not, as the case may be) or even told it was time to go!

But deep down I was embarrassed by his behaviour and hurt that even people who knew what he'd been through could still stare and say nothing. In fact, any comment would have been better that none!

Anyway, we plodded on and I got better and stronger at coping with and ignoring offending behaviour from both Robert and our onlookers. So we could, to all intents and purposes, say that all was well, but then Jennifer's behaviour began to deteriorate into episodes of whining and whingeing and generally being very irritable. I thought at first this may have been in response to all the attention being directed towards Robert, although we had always tried to divide out time, attention and love equally, while being aware that at certain times this was just not proving to work completely. However, we thought that most of the time we were doing a pretty good job of sharing ourselves equally.

In desperation, I called the health visitor for some advice. She came to the house immediately and reassured me that she actually did not think Jennifer's behaviour was a result of our handling of the situation (past or present). Funnily enough, though, I was

And Then There Were Three

more than surprised when she suggested we have Jennifer's hearing checked! I had never given it a thought but she pointed out that after Robert's hearing problems this might not be a bad idea.

I don't know if I was more relieved or worried, as it turned out that Jennifer did indeed have a similar problem with poor hearing (although not to the extent that Robert did) and that she too in fact had enormous tonsils! So what had seemed to us like bad behaviour was simply the fact that she wasn't hearing too well and was probably in quite a lot of discomfort. It appeared that Jennifer's problems could be sorted quite easily with the same operation Robert had had.

The consultant's registrar saw Jennifer and described how quick and simple the operation was and how there was no need to worry. He, of course, knew nothing of the problems our son had had during the same 'simple' operation.

Of course I did worry. I went to my sister's to pick up Robert and I cried again. Part of me was relieved while part of me was desperate. 'What should I do?' I asked Jan. 'Do I let her have the operation or not?'

Could I live with myself if I signed the consent form and something went wrong? But I knew deep down that I had made up my mind.

Jennifer was suffering and I knew the chances of anything similar happening again were very remote. I had to let her have the operation. How could I make a decision that would leave her struggling and suffering?

Two weeks after her fourth birthday, Jennifer had her operation. I stayed with her and we were in for two days. How I cried over those two days, but I never let her see.

All went well, though, I have to say, and I have never been so relieved as when they wheeled her back into the ward. I knew it was Jennifer even though I couldn't see her face. All I could see was her lovely long brown hair. I cried again as we settled her into her bed. My husband said, 'Now what are you crying for?' Will men ever understand the emotions of women? I was crying with joy. I was so happy I thought, It's all over. Neither of them has any tonsils or adenoids now to be a problem. We can get on and enjoy life.

And Then There Were Three

Jennifer was an absolute angel while we were in the hospital. She loved the attention and wasn't a bit bothered about the op! She boasted that she was having the same operation as her brother and didn't mind taking any medicine at all. She does like her sleep, though; one sedative and she was out for the count. She was quite put out that she hadn't seen the operating suite!

I was so proud of Jennifer. She behaved beautifully and her health and happiness improved dramatically from that moment on. She was back to the old Jennifer. Such an enthusiastic child and so eager to learn and please. She seemed to cope extremely well with all the changes life threw at her.

Two weeks after her operation, Jennifer started school at the tender age of four years and one month (this being due to the government changes). Again, she coped brilliantly and was of course the most beautiful little angel of them all!

She stood in line with thirty other boys and girls, all dressed in their new uniforms. She had two long brown plaits in her hair and a beaming grin. Her pinafore was miles too long and her plimsoll bag dragged along the floor, but she looked beautiful!

While all this was going on (as if that wasn't enough) we moved house to cope with our ever-growing family! Yes, you guessed. Shortly before Jennifer's operation, we discovered that I was expecting our third child! Perhaps this accounts slightly for some of my emotional outbursts!

I think it happened around Robert's second birthday. Despite the problems of Robert's early years, we had always wanted three or four children. We loved Jennifer and Robert dearly but we couldn't decide whether or not to have another child. Should we give all our attention to our two youngsters (much needed by our son, but just how much we were still unaware of) or should we have another? We both loved having babies and toddlers around the house and as Robert progressed from cot to bed, it seemed he really wasn't a baby any more. We'd looked at the empty cot and wondered what it would be like having just one more!

We couldn't make up our minds what to do so we decided to do nothing. We decided to leave it to Mother Nature or the powers that be and see what happened. Bearing in mind it took seven months of trying to conceive both Jennifer and Robert, we weren't exactly expecting results for months! Of course, when you least expect it these things have a way of happening, don't they? So after just one month, we found ourselves preparing to cope with the arrival of another baby. I must say, however, that we were delighted that the decision seemed to have been made for us. We decided it was obviously meant to be, as it just happened, and we were overjoyed. In a way, it was probably a blessing in disguise because had we perhaps waited a year or two or discovered the extent of Robert's problems, then maybe we wouldn't have had another baby, and we certainly wouldn't have missed having Catherine for the world. She is wonderful.

The pregnancy, the birth and Catherine's first year went so quickly. Right from the start, everything seemed to happen so fast; presumably this was because, this being the third time around and already having a demanding young family to look after, one doesn't have much time to dwell on looking after oneself or looking to the future. We just had to get on with everything, and before we knew it, we were driving to the nursing home with only twenty-nine minutes to spare before the somewhat hasty arrival of our second baby girl. This time I got my wish. My son is so special, I wanted to keep him special, and yes, deep down I still secretly wanted to have two girls. I can't explain this but I was ecstatic. I felt my family was perfect. Two girls and a boy – who could wish for more?

Catherine arrived in the world as she intended to carry on: just like a whirlwind. Everything went so quickly. She fitted into family life perfectly. I suppose you might say she had to. She had to learn to take her place in the family, and sometimes she may have had to wait a little longer than a first baby might for something, but she didn't seem to mind. She was always so content, she was a pleasure from the moment she arrived. We called her our little treasure. Maybe some of her behaviour reflected a more relaxed attitude, a more confident approach from her parents. I have to say, after each child I learnt to be a little more patient and relaxed about things. You have to be, otherwise you'd be saying 'no' all the time or tearing your hair out.

Despite Robert's behaviour, we were determined (having seen how quickly the children were growing up) that we were going to enjoy every minute of Catherine's first year. So although Robert may have been a handful, we can look back and say that we did indeed enjoy Catherine throughout her first year.

I fed her myself for longer than I did Robert. I kept thinking I'd better make the most of it, just in case she was our last. She took to breastfeeding beautifully and I enjoyed the feeling of closeness. Despite the tiredness, I fed her for about seven months and was quite sad when it came to that last feed. Catherine, however, made the decision to give up breastfeeding easier for me. She more or less decided herself that it was time to give up. As she took more bottles and more solids she became less interested in the breast, so we came to a mutual agreement and stopped. I must admit, I didn't feel half so tired but I still missed feeding her.

While writing this chapter, Catherine was asleep and my recollections of her days at that time were of a tiny bundle of fun. She was petite and looked like she should be a delicate, dainty little girl, but she was and is far from this. My husband joked that we had a girl, a boy and a monkey!

Catherine did everything early: she crawled, sat and walked well before the expected age. She was into everything. We found a trail of destruction wherever she went. She wandered from room to room with a mischievous grin on her face, deciding what she could get up to next. Everybody commented about her smile and the funny faces she could pull. She was always smiling, she was so content.

I have to say that Catherine had quite a character and certainly kept everybody amused. I never ceased to be amazed by the things she did; she really was a joy to have around. I hope I am right in saying that the rest of the family were also just as pleased with her as we were, even if she was a bit of a surprise.

Jennifer and Robert never seemed a bit put out by her arrival either. They quite simply adored her, and she likewise adored them.

As I have often said, it's a good job she came along when she did; we wouldn't be without her for the world. We wouldn't be without any of them!

Is Anybody Listening?

About a month after Catherine was born, Robert started playschool. He started at the new lower age of two years and nine months. It became increasingly apparent, once Robert was mixing regularly with children of his own age, that all was not well. It is surprising how quickly one forgets what is expected in the normal development of young children and I had again not appreciated the differences between the progress of girls and boys. In the past few hectic months, I had also tried to put Robert's problems aside and had begun to think (as everyone kept telling me) that he would soon catch up and gradually outgrow some of his more bizarre behaviour.

It was by now, however, becoming too obvious that Robert was falling far behind the standards expected in playschool, and while one is advised not to make comparisons with other children, it is of course extremely difficult not to.

I had tried not to compare Robert too much to Jennifer at his age (for one thing, I found it difficult to recall exactly how she was at this age) because she was, in fact, quite forward and I did not expect the same from a boy. Seeing Robert mixing with other boys, in particular in his group, I had to admit that by now Robert was performing at a much lower level than even I had anticipated. Obviously I knew he would be a little bit behind following his earlier traumatic years, but I was surprised to find that all of a sudden I was reminded of the seriousness of his problems. More importantly, I realised that I really should be trying to help him somehow, but how? I just didn't know what to do for the best.

I decided to wait a while and see if he settled down now that he was attending playschool regularly. Things did not settle down, though, and when the playschool supervisor suggested that they could get a special needs assistant in playschool for Robert, I knew that I had to do something.

Other people, professional people, were beginning to notice

that there was something not quite right. Robert had, by this time, been in playschool for a few months and his behavioural skills, social skills and language development were not improving at all; in fact, I have to say that at this time I thought Robert was getting worse by the day. The bigger he got, the more difficult he got. I knew that in our local authority the three-year development checks carried out by the health visitor were actually being done at approximately three and a half years. This was probably due to the fact that the increase in population was making it impossible for an already overstretched medical practice to test all children on time.

Having concerns about Robert's development I approached the health visitor and asked her if she could do his development check as soon as possible. I explained that there were some aspects of Robert's development that were causing us great concern so she agreed to come and assess him at home in two weeks.

When the health visitor came to the house, I felt initially that she thought we were wasting her time. She started to do some standard development checks and it was clear almost immediately that Robert was unable to complete the tasks expected of him. Alison (our health visitor) suggested that we should perhaps wait a further six months and then reassess Robert. Again I began to panic. I thought, No! There's something wrong with him and he needs help now, not in six months' time.

In fact 'we' also needed help now. I was beginning to feel desperate, and in fact totally and utterly shattered from the constant battling just to get through normal everyday activities with Robert. Anyway, Alison must have sensed something because she explained that in a further six months Robert may have caught up a bit more and may perform much better at the assessment. Alison also reminded me about the differences between the progress rates of boys and girls and the fact that they were still testing most children at three and a half. However, she carried on with the assessment and listened to my concerns. She seemed quite surprised when I explained the difficulties we were having just getting through the day with so many tantrums.

As she tested him further, luckily she became more aware herself of the seriousness of the problem and in fact changed her

Is Anybody Listening?

approach totally. She said then that it was a good job we had called her when we did, as there was (as I had always said) something definitely not right with Robert, but she did not have the answers. She suggested a few tactics to help avoid some of the tantrums and then recommended that Robert be assessed by the clinical medical officer from the child development team. As she left the house, I at least felt reassured that we weren't making a fuss over nothing, but was nevertheless a bit disappointed that we didn't have something more concrete to go on right then!

So again I watched for the post every morning, hoping for a little brown envelope with 'NHS' stamped on the outside! Of course, eventually an appointment arrived through the post and on the day Robert and I set off, not quite sure what to expect next. In fact, the doctor performed exactly the same assessment as the health visitor and by now I was actually beginning to anticipate their next move. She listened to Robert's history and did the same practical tests that I knew he was unable to do. As expected, Robert performed rather poorly and I simply became more exhausted watching him struggle, willing him to do something. I wanted to speak to him and help with the tests, but I knew I had to watch and wait to see if he could do any for himself.

The doctor actually didn't see any of the more aggressive, wilder aspects of his behaviour but instead got the more introverted, shy and extremely negative side of him. Robert failed further in the language tests, as he refused to say a word that day. The test lasted two hours and by the end I felt totally exhausted and Robert seemed a little bit bewildered as he insisted on cuddling for hours afterwards.

As expected, the doctor explained that there was an obvious delay in Robert's development and suggested he might benefit from some extra help on a one to one basis. Of course, first she said he would have to be assessed by the educational psychologist! I knew by now that Robert would be asked to perform the same tasks again for somebody different and that we had ahead of us more waiting and more uncertainty! We still as yet had no clues as to what was wrong with Robert, if indeed there was anything, and to what degree of severity. We also had no idea of what we could or could not expect for his future. People kept telling me to be patient and advising me that no one could tell us anything yet, as nobody had the answers themselves and that it really was still only early days. However, it didn't seem like early days when your whole existence seemed to be taken up with trying to placate an extremely difficult child and maintain some degree of peace in the home.

So again we went home and got on with the daily battles while waiting for a further appointment. This time, the doctor came to the house. I arranged for Mike's mum to have Catherine so we would not be distracted further. This was a good move as the psychologist was with us for three hours! As expected, the tests were much the same but a little more in-depth. The psychologist listened carefully to what I had to say and was very patient with both Robert in his performance (or not, in most cases) of tasks and myself as by now I was becoming desperate for some answers and also some solutions to our problems. She reassured me that I was not imagining things and that Robert's problems were not due to parental handling of situations, this being a great relief! However, she had to admit that she could not give us more definite answers right now but did give us some hope. She suggested that a definite period of assessment in a special nursery would be of much benefit to Robert and us.

The doctor made an appointment for us to see the special school with Robert to decide for ourselves if we were happy for him to attend. She left the house and this time I felt we had at least been given something definite to aim for. We were going to be able to get some help and advice and now maybe even some answers as to the cause of the problems. As always, though, my feelings were torn equally between positive and negative. I was beginning to feel that there really was something wrong with my precious son. I know I had been pressing for some time now for help and some acknowledgement of the problem, but maybe half of me was quite happy all the time there was some uncertainty. I had always known deep down that there was something wrong; it just seemed sort of final now that the professionals were agreeing and had recommended Robert for special education.

Alison had been in regular contact since our first meeting and was being very supportive, merely by showing concern and

Is Anybody Listening?

phoning regularly to see how we were getting on. Mike, being self-employed and recently out of work, found it difficult to take time off for appointments, as with our growing family, although not on the poverty line, we were limited to quite a strict budget. Thus, faced with the prospect of viewing the special school on my own with Robert and Catherine in tow, I didn't hesitate when Alison offered to come with me. A little bit of company and moral support goes a long way!

The school was lovely, and the staff certainly seemed to be dedicated to the children in their care. I saw many examples of enormous patience yet very definite discipline, obviously much needed while aiming to care for and teach children like Robert. From what I could see, there were other children with similar problems to Robert, some a little better, some a little worse. This was reassuring as it reminded me that we weren't alone; there were other children and other parents who must be going through similar experiences to us.

I knew I had already made up my mind that Robert needed the help and we would be accepting the place offered to him but I found it impossible to say it! Just to say yes when asked if we'd like a place for our son seemed like such an enormous hurdle. It was probably the first hurdle in accepting for ourselves that our son had a problem. The teacher showing us round was very sensitive; she simply suggested that we should go away and talk about it and then we could contact the school when we'd made our decision.

Alison went back to work and Robert and I went home for lunch. For the first time ever I felt numb. I couldn't think straight, let alone talk. Every time I thought of anything I found myself crying again. I prayed that for once the phone wouldn't ring. I didn't feel like talking to anyone as I was too emotional. I think it was seeing all the little boys and girls in the school and realising that Robert wasn't really that much different to them. Robert really did need the help and so did we. Now at last it was being offered, so why couldn't I say yes?

Well, of course, after speaking with Mike I wrote to the school accepting Robert's place. He was to start in the January term for three full days a week.

Having prepared oneself for one's offspring leaving the security of home and not being entirely dependent on their parents the whole time at about four or five years old, I felt a bit like I was losing my son to someone else's care far sooner than anticipated. Why on earth are mothers so emotional? Are we doomed to feel guilty whichever decisions we make for our children? Any amount of reassurance that I was doing the right thing didn't help, either. I could reason with myself until the cows came home but I simply felt like I was sending my little boy away.

However, yet again I had to pull myself together and be strong for the whole family. Of course I was doing the right thing. We all needed the help and I was certainly not going to deprive Robert of any chance of help from the professionals, if he was going to have any hope of attending mainstream school and learning well in the future.

Over the next few weeks, I tried hard to be extra patient with Robert (pangs of guilt creeping in, no doubt) but found this increasingly difficult. Robert was so difficult to direct in his tasks and extremely negative. Every little thing seemed to take so long and there were many tantrums.

There were eight weeks to go until Robert started in the special needs nursery, and although I knew I was going to miss him dreadfully, the eight weeks suddenly seemed like an eternity. With every day becoming more of a battle and Robert also growing much bigger and much more physical by the day, I was becoming less tolerant of the children in general and felt constantly tired and irritable. I think at one stage I lost my confidence with all the children. I didn't know what to do for the best with Jennifer or Robert and was questioning everything I did for the baby. I began to doubt my own capabilities, especially with the baby, which is silly in a way because I found this stage easier by far than the older children; after all, I'd already had two babies before Catherine! We became like prisoners in our own home for a while, as I was embarrassed by Robert's behaviour and too ashamed even to have friends into the house. I think I should have been more embarrassed and ashamed that I even felt like this; it wasn't Robert's fault and we were only doing our best with him.

Is Anybody Listening?

So apart from the necessary school run for Jennifer and playschool for Robert, we stayed indoors. By now it was even too cold to play in the garden.

After a while, I must have picked up a bit, though, because I remember thinking, I don't want to be cooped up indoors – I want to go out! So we did go out.

I regained my confidence and thought, So what if people stare if Robert has a tantrum. I knew he wasn't just a naughty boy, I knew he was special, so we had simply to go out there together and get on with life, get on with living. We obviously found ways of making shopping trips and waiting in the school playground for Jennifer a little easier, but every outing was still pretty exhausting though at least we were out more. I took to using the double buggy, although Robert was much too big for this, and it had the desired effect of restraining him with a reasonable amount of dignity for shopping trips. I always tried to reward a reasonably calm trip with a visit to the swings afterwards to burn up some of Robert's energy and show him that he could soon have time to play. Shopping trips or visits to friends and family had to be planned with a certain degree of military precision. Organisation was paramount to enable a reasonable trip out without provoking too much bizarre behaviour, thus leaving Mummy wondering why she bothered! This went well for a while but soon Robert really was too big (and heavy) to push in the double buggy so we transferred to walking with reigns on! Not quite so successful but we managed.

I still felt that Robert's behaviour was getting worse by the day. Maybe it was just that some of the more physical behaviour was more obvious as Robert was growing so rapidly now. He seemed to be knocking into things more indoors and became generally clumsier. He also seemed much more disruptive and aggressive during and immediately after playschool sessions.

I can remember one particularly bad outburst of embarrassing behaviour when we visited our local chemist one afternoon. It was just before we were due at school to pick up Jennifer. Catherine was in the buggy and Robert was on reins. Robert was touching or grabbing at everything in sight. I tried very discreetly

Is Anybody Listening?

to say a firm and definite no, to which onlookers might just as well have thought I'd begun World War Three.

Robert threw himself on the floor and started to kick and scream. It was obvious he was not going to be placated. A few months earlier I would have picked him up, tucked him under my arm and marched off, buggy and all. But Robert really was now much too heavy for me to do this. Added to which, in these instances he had an amazing ability to become impossibly limp! So what should I do? Drag him off and force him to walk by holding the reins at body point (extremely undignified and humiliating for us both) or sit it out (also extremely undignified and humiliating, although a lot less physical)? Sitting it out with Robert, however, could take anywhere between ten minutes and an hour, both of which seemed like an eternity.

I felt much too tired to do battle anyway so I busied myself with looking at displays, chatting to Catherine (who probably thought it all a wonderful show) and generally trying to pretend that I, or Robert, or both, were on another planet. This act of trying to be cheerful and patient was also extremely exhausting, so as soon as we reached the car my silly grin slipped from my face as I slumped, exhausted and relieved into the driver's seat. I knew that for some ten minutes until we arrived at school Robert was at least safe and restrained in his car seat, where he couldn't do too much harm. I just tried to ignore the noise and hope that ten minutes was sufficient to achieve a certain degree of calm and to compose myself before arriving at school.

Another incident I must write about before I forget altogether (because this is, in fact, more recent so quite out of sequence now) was another equally embarrassing and exhausting display. However, even I had to laugh at this one before we had left the scene, as it actually appealed to my bizarre sense of humour.

We were at my mother-in-law's church for a special service for Mother's Day. Robert was being generally disruptive and clumsy and drawing attention to our pew, but unless he was actually going to hurt someone or break something I thought it best not to intervene. Knowing Robert, this would have provoked a disastrous response, drawing even more attention to our family. So again I put on my silly grin, looked everywhere but at Robert

Is Anybody Listening?

and sang my heart out to the hymns (very calming). So we managed reasonably, with our three children, four adult family members and another two young cousins. Not too bad, you could say, however, the bomb had to drop at some point!

The time came to leave the relative safety of the pew and walk up the aisle for Holy Communion or a blessing. As Robert's recent history of behaviour had been pretty appalling, I was determined that he was going to get more than his fair share of blessing! Anything short of a miracle seemed appropriate at that precise moment, but Robert became equally determined that there was no way he was going anywhere near the vicar for a blessing. So here we go again! My brain asked, do we go or do we stay? Well, as I thought he was in desperate need of his blessing that day, there was no choice. Catherine wouldn't go with anyone but me that day and no one else was willing to be seen up the aisle with Robert, so off we went, Catherine on one arm and Robert by the collar, kicking and screaming. I think (I hope), the vicar saw the funny side and placed his hands on Robert's head. At the same moment I raised my eyes to the sky and whispered, 'Please give him a bigger share today!' The amazing thing was the rest of the family said that they hadn't even noticed.

This incident being slightly out of sequence, I must return to the point. With Robert's behaviour deteriorating quite noticeably, we had about eight weeks to go before the Christmas break and then Robert starting at special school in January. At playschool, Robert seemed to wander aimlessly between activities. The staff couldn't be blamed as they were not trained to deal with children like this. They could not direct him to do anything constructive or creative without provoking a scene so they merely let him play. However, he would become more and more boisterous and come home quite high and disruptive.

I was explaining this point one afternoon on the phone to a friend, and she suggested I contact the vicar's wife in a nearby parish who ran an opportunities group.

The group was a much smaller playgroup catering for local children but with places for children with special needs. My friend explained that being halfway through the school term, it was highly unlikely that there would be any places available but

Robert's first birthday

Jennifer's first day at school

Robert's first day at school

Jennifer, Robert and Catherine. Young love!

*The children relaxing in Spain,
the first holiday abroad*

Jennifer and Robert at toddler group

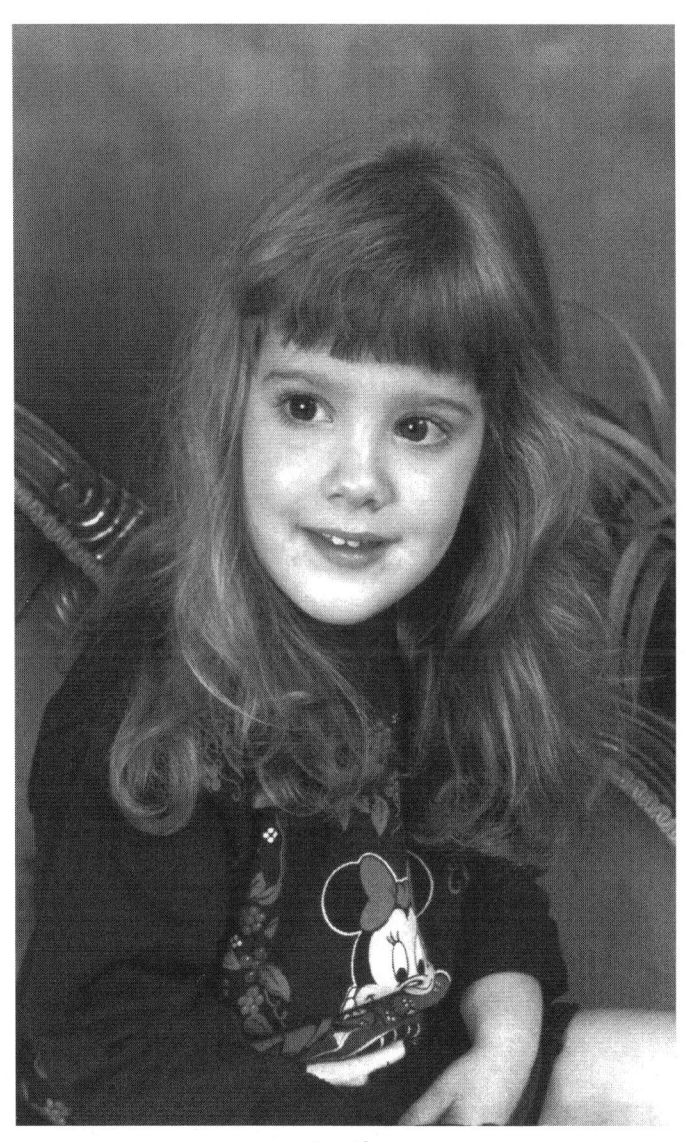

Jennifer

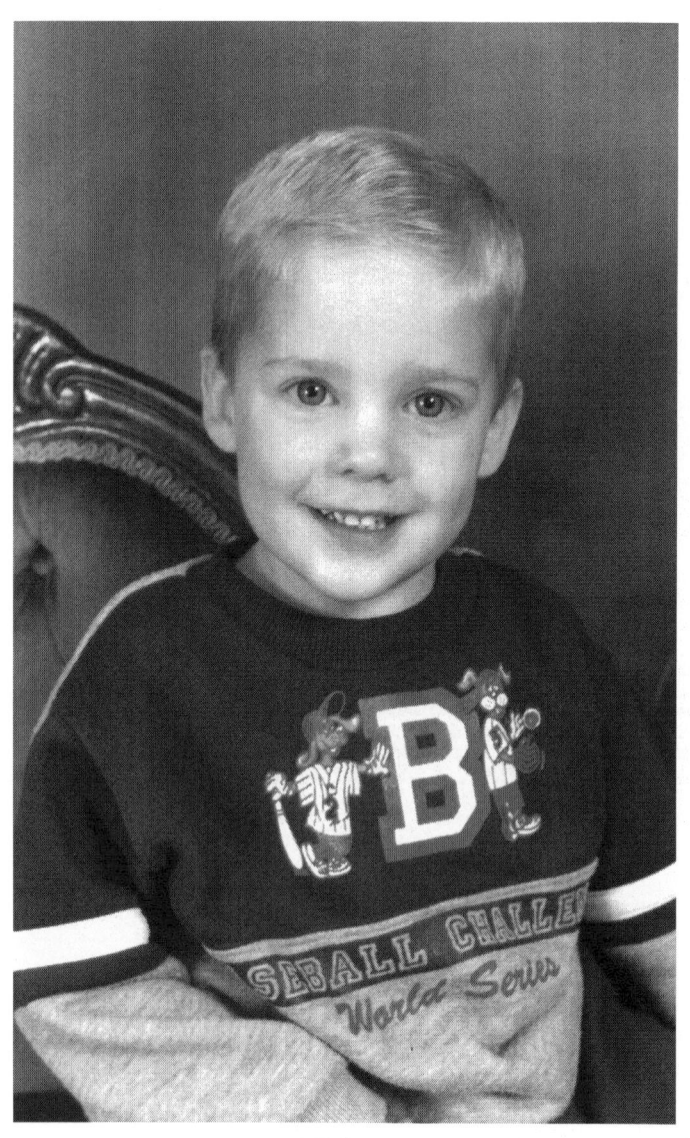

Robert

Catherine

Jennifer

Robert

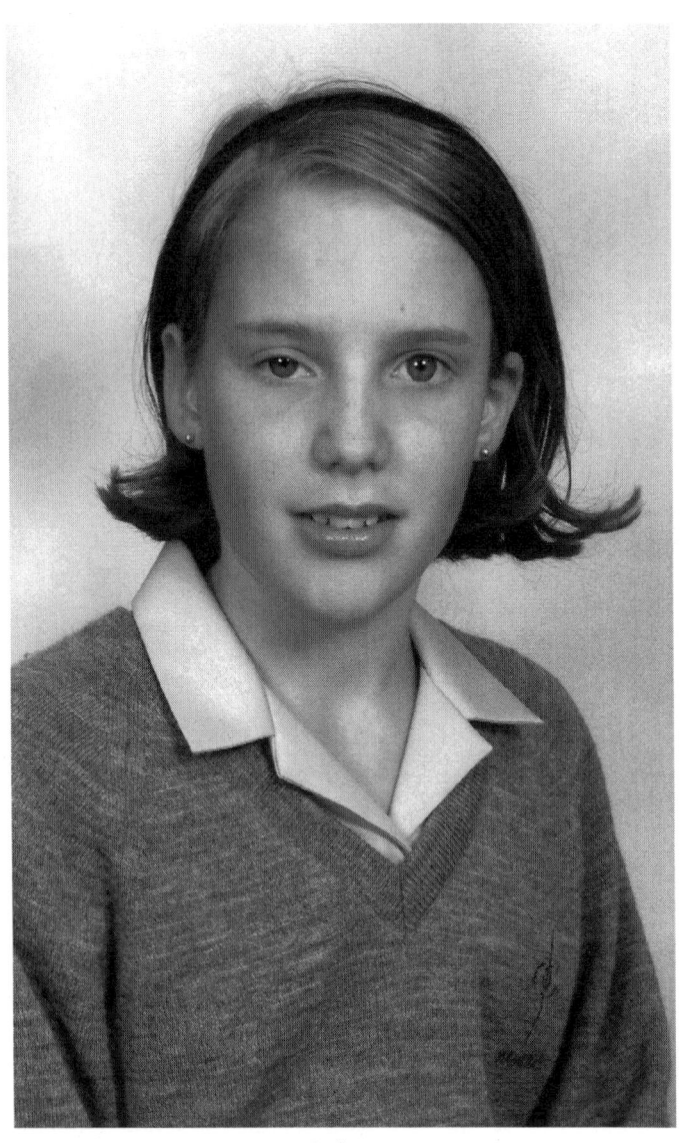

Catherine

Jennifer, Robert and Catherine together at after-school club while Mum was in hospital – still smiling!

Angels all round!

suggested calling her anyway as she may be able to provide us with advice or information. Not only did she think she could provide me with professional assistance, but also with some practical tips as she herself had fostered several children with Down's syndrome.

Well, I did contact the vicar's wife and to my astonishment she said she had a place available to start immediately! She suggested I take Robert to the group the very next week to meet her and see what we all thought. So I made arrangements for Catherine to stay with her gran and Robert and I spent a wonderful morning together at the group. The staff were lovely. They were so softly spoken, calm and patient, yet they followed some very stringent discipline regimes (I wish I could strike this balance). Robert's response was amazing; he was still difficult to direct and negative but I couldn't expect too much as I was still with him and it was all very new to him. However, he was much quieter and calmer. He sat nicely for drinks and biscuits and played beautifully in their garden. He seemed to take very well to the vicar's wife (as did all the children) and even sat with the others in a circle for song time, although his participation was yet underdeveloped.

Robert was much calmer at home too that afternoon (as compared to his other playschool days) and as he had been offered the place to begin immediately, my mind was made up. I drafted a letter to his old group removing him from their register. Obviously this was quite emotional as Jennifer and Robert had both attended this particular group, but I had to think of Robert's needs, indeed the needs of the entire family for the future. My health visitor said that they did not usually advocate changing playgroups, but, in this case they agreed that I had made the right decision.

Obviously the first morning I left him at the opportunity group he cried as I left, but I was reassured that it was all for my benefit and stopped within five minutes. When I picked him up from that very first session, for the first time ever Robert came home with some craftwork! He had drawn and painted, as had the other children. He hadn't been given choices, you see, simply told that everybody sits down to do a drawing! I was so proud! Robert's work then hung from our dining-room walls as

Jennifer's always had and it was lovely to see. Obviously, Robert hadn't transformed into an angel overnight, but the point I think I am trying to make is that change can occur with the right kind of help. Robert still had tantrums and still had days when nothing went right, but he was also learning some things, even small things like discipline, sharing and participating. These are things, you may well say, that we should have taught him, but he seemed far more willing to take discipline from anyone but the family. Robert's learning, his progress, was very slow but it was nevertheless progress. I remain completely convinced that this was one decision I got totally correct!

After a few sessions, Robert could walk quite nicely to their garden holding hands, could produce craftwork, could play constructively alongside other children and if not join in with their singing, he would at least sit in the circle for song time. After a few months Robert's memory was beginning to show signs of developing and he would sing recognisable snippets of nursery rhymes at home!

I will end this chapter on a light note as, despite all that had happened, I have always maintained that humour and laughter are an ideal tonic.

At the playgroup, the children sang a song about a worm that goes something like this:

> There's a worm at the bottom of my garden
> And his name is Wiggly Woo.
> He wiggles to the left, he wiggles to the right,
> He wiggles all day and he wiggles all night.
> There's a worm at the bottom of my garden
> And his name is Wiggly Woo.

Having established that Jennifer also knew this song, we were delighted that here was a song our children could share together. There are, of course, appropriate actions to go with the rhyme. Sadly Robert's memory was not developing as well as would be expected. Robert could only remember very limited numbers of words or activities in sequence, this presumably inhibiting his learning processes. In this instance, in particular though, one has

Is Anybody Listening?

to laugh, as Robert's version of the song, no matter how hard we tried to teach him, went something like this:

> There's a worm at my bottom
> And his name said Wiggy Wiggy Woo!

Help!

Shortly after Robert started at the new playgroup, I read an article about hyperactive children and diet. The symptoms listed seemed to describe Robert perfectly, although he also had many more problems than those identified. I think Robert's situation would have been easier for us to cope with if he had a definite diagnosis. Even if Robert had an obvious disability, it would have been easier for us to come to terms with, and perhaps we would have accepted things more readily. As it was, Robert was said to have 'special needs' and was referred to 'special school' for a more thorough assessment period.

I myself am not sure if Robert is hyperactive or not, although I must agree that some of the symptoms bore a striking resemblance to those suffered by our son. However, Robert also had other problems to contend with, and if my memory serves me well, one assessment described him as having a moderate learning disability with developmental delay. The 'in phrase' at the moment for hyperactive children seems to be 'attention deficit and hyperactivity disorder', rather a posh new name for an old-fashioned but poorly recognised condition. Robert's list of problems, when asked to describe, could take one a long time to discuss, hence when asked by friends or other mums at Jennifer's school why Robert was in special school or what was wrong with him it was impossible to give a clear, concise answer. One either had to begin a very long-winded explanation of his history, or simply say, 'Oh he's just a bit behind!' Neither of these really answered the question though, did it?

In America, attention deficit and hyperactivity disorder is much more widely recognised than in Britain. Why is it that our doctors are so reluctant to diagnose? Having read about the famous Feingold diet (and also having put it into practice years earlier while working with severely disabled children), I decided, as every mum would probably agree, that even though I wasn't

Help!

too convinced as to the success of the diet, I really was desperate and felt I myself should be doing something for my son. Any mother or father surely feels that they must try everything if there is the slightest chance of it helping their child. I had also heard of doctors who specialised in allergy testing. I thought it would be a good idea to have Robert tested for allergies before embarking on a quite complicated and restrictive diet. After all, there's surely no point avoiding substances unnecessarily if no allergy has been proved. This also seemed a good step, as being asthmatic (also often triggered by allergens) and being unable to tolerate formula milk as a baby, it seemed sensible to find out what, if anything, Robert was allergic to.

I approached my GP and asked if he would refer Robert to a specialist for allergy testing. I was totally astonished and taken aback when he quite simply refused to refer him. I feel at this point I should also mention that the GP, knowing the extent of Robert's problems (I presume he read his copies of all Robert's assessments) and knowing the family pretty well too, I thought, had not once suggested that a referral to a paediatrician would be a good idea.

Looking back now, I can't believe I overlooked this point. It wasn't until he started at special school that the doctor conducting Robert's medical suggested that it was time for a referral and did the honours herself. We were finally going to see a paediatrician with Robert and maybe get some definite answers.

I sincerely hope that this reluctance to refer people 'generally' to a chosen specialist is not an indication of the direction in which our health service is moving. After all, referrals cost money, don't they? Maybe a fund-holding practice is nowadays not too keen on having people with long-term conditions on its books, or are more and more problems simply being dismissed and swept under the carpet, thus leaving patients and carers struggling to cope, unsupported and uninformed?

Political views aside, I was stunned by our GP's comments and too shocked at the time to retaliate. He suggested that Robert's problems were all behavioural, that having a fancy name for a diagnosis would not help the situation, and that the diet was proved in many cases to be a waste of time. Maybe this latter

Help!

point I might have been inclined to agree with him on; however, I felt he was being rather insensitive to my feelings and a little too hasty to offer personal opinions. As a professional, I would have expected a little more diplomacy. I'm sure all doctors have different ideas and preferences on all forms of treatments and medications for all conditions, including alternative medicine. Far be it for them to advocate only their treatment of personal choice. I began to feel as if I had asked for the world and felt as small as a snail as I crawled home with the three children in tow. I'm sure you can imagine the scene: three young children and me in the doctor's surgery, the children all vying for attention, myself trying to hold a decent conversation with the doctor while actually feeling totally desperate. Perhaps I was being a little too naive, but I had expected a certain degree of sympathy, the GP also being a father of three young children! I had also hoped that he would anticipate the desperation we were now feeling and I must admit I was rather disappointed that he failed in this (I've probably been watching too much *Peak Practice*).

I too can be sympathetic though and make allowances for probably an overstretched, overworked and underpaid service (sorry, no more politics) but when your child is suffering and life is generally becoming such a trial, it is very difficult not to be angry. I went home and cried again, partly because I was so angry and partly because I felt very let down and unsupported. At this point I was very, very low. I could see no end in sight.

Thankfully, the next day our health visitor called to see how we were and restored my faith in human kindness and indeed the health service. She did agree that perhaps the GP had been a little hasty in his decision and really ought to have kept his personal opinion to himself. She also reassured me that we were in fact coping tremendously well and said she thought I was doing a wonderful job. Having raised my self-esteem and confidence again, at least to the level it was before our visit to the surgery, she suggested that I leave the problem with her for a few days and she would find me some literature on the subject.

True to her word, as always, she returned a few days later armed with booklets and leaflets for us to read at our leisure. Well, I did read the leaflets, but my husband and I, with a little

Help!

assistance from my father, had already decided that we would pay privately for Robert to have his allergy test. We couldn't really afford the extra money, but again, when your child is suffering you will try anything. Having no referral, we took Robert to the lady who ran the local hyperactive children's support group for some general advice and an alternative allergy test.

Again, I must admit that I wasn't convinced. The lady, being a herbalist, tested Robert for allergies by placing test tubes containing common substances against Robert's skin. At the same time, she explained that she was feeling for reactions of muscle tension in Robert's arm. Having been trained in physical medicine, I was a little sceptical as I could see no physical evidence myself of any reaction to any substances. However, after the test the lady produced an impressively long list of substances she said Robert had reacted to. The list included all sugars, chocolate, cow's milk, cheese, white flour, yeast, oranges, tomatoes and most food colourings; most of the basic ingredients really in our daily diet. This meant a drastic and costly change to at least Robert's eating habits and maybe also our other children. After all, you can't give sweets to one child in front of another who really doesn't understand and simply say 'You can't have any', can you? This, surely, is a recipe for disaster. So we thought perhaps it would do us all good to go back to the old-fashioned ways a little and have a more basic but healthy diet. We all ate more vegetables and fruit and we bought goat's milk and cheese for Robert and a few 'special treats' from our local health shop. I drew the line at baking with wholemeal flour, so we bought special biscuits and avoided cakes and pies. We made much more of an effort to make casseroles and eat pasta and rice dishes, so generally I think we became more conscious of our own dietary intake and Robert was having very close to the Feingold diet and he really didn't seem too bothered by it all.

Robert actually has a wonderful appetite. He simply adores food, any food, and as long as we filled him up regularly, he didn't seem to mind what he ate.

The diet did prove to be more expensive and we let Robert (and ourselves) have a couple of days off over Christmas. After a month or so there really was no change in Robert at all, so we

Help!

gradually reintroduced 'banned' substances until he was generally having a more normal diet. We can at least say that we tried it, and if nothing else it had made us generally eat a much healthier range of foods and be more aware of what we ate.

At about the same time as starting at the new playgroup, Robert also started attending a language progress group. This group was run by Robert's speech therapist, whom he was seeing at approximately three-monthly intervals. I had always thought that this was a bit inadequate as Robert was certainly getting enough conversation and encouragement with his communication skills at home. Therefore, if he was going to have speech therapy I had always thought it would be much better if it was a little more frequent. This would at least enable Robert to become familiar with his speech therapist; after all, if he was to communicate at all with anybody he needed first to build up a trusting relationship. So, as was usually the case, Robert attempted very little speech at all during these three monthly sessions.

However, we had to put a certain degree of faith and trust in the professionals and I had to accept her recommendations at the time. Needless to say, when she suggested that Robert attend the progress group, I was much more optimistic and thought it would be more appropriate for Robert! I think she had to agree that his speech in fact was not progressing as expected.

So I began to take Robert to the progress group, once a week on a Monday morning. The session was for about an hour and a half and there would be about seven or eight children in the group, all with speech or language problems. The speech therapist had a special needs assistant with her and the mums took turns at watching for one session each. This was quite a unique experience, actually being able to watch the professionals at work with our children. I must say, I was certainly impressed again by the degree of patience of these amazing women.

In no time at all, Robert settled into the group and was more than happy to be left, as far as he seemed aware, simply to play with his new friends for a while. At the end of each session, the mums were invited into an adjoining room to discuss with the therapist and each other their children's progress and their performance that morning. This was also quite a new experience;

Help!

for the first time ever I met other mums who were experiencing difficulties with their children. How wonderful it was comparing notes and exchanging stories.

Robert did indeed seem to progress well in this group. When he first joined, he was still saying mostly one word on its own, whether trying to make a statement, ask for something he wanted, or answer a question. After just a few weeks he started to put two words together like 'Daddy home' or 'Juice, please'. Once Robert got the hang of this, he simply raced along, joining two, three, even four words together. It was really quite an amazing thing to watch; in just a few months, Robert became another incessant chatterbox (there's a lot of them in our family) and he seemed delighted with his new-found skill. The understanding of language and the ability to communicate are such wonderful gifts, but I'm sure most of us probably take them for granted.

Robert's time in this group, however, was short-lived; he left after only one term as he was to start at his special school and would be having regular speech therapy there. I am grateful for the time Robert was given by the speech therapy team and am delighted that this again proved to have been another decision I will never regret.

So, in January 1996, Robert started at Heathfield Special School in Fareham. The week before I busied myself preparing for his first day. I made sure he had his bag ready with clean clothes (in case of accidents), and hurriedly sewed name tags into all his clothes and anything else that would be going with him.

His first day wasn't as traumatic as I had anticipated. The first week, I took Robert to school myself. I'm sure that his past experience of changing playgroups and going to the progress group all helped to make this transition easier. I think that maybe Robert just thought this was similar to playgroup; he had no concept of time, so he probably wasn't too aware that he was staying much longer. The fact that he was given a cooked meal in the middle of the day, I'm sure, would have been a bonus, loving food as he did. The first week was probably more emotional for me than for him. He came home very excited, but also very tired the first day. He seemed eager to return the next day, too, this making the settling-in period much easier for all concerned.

Help!

Robert was to attend for three days a week initially. This was quite sufficient as he was still also to go to his playgroup once a week. We had one full day a week home together and we very quickly made this 'our special day'. The teachers reported that Robert was settling in well and I was reassured that again we had made the right decision. However, the second week was to prove far from easy.

As Robert had been recommended for special education, the council were to provide transport to and from school. A taxi was arranged to pick Robert up from home on the second Monday, and to take him to school and bring him home each day thereafter. I had deliberately requested that I take Robert myself the first week to help settle him in. I also thought that it would help when getting in the taxi if he knew where he was going. This second Monday was definitely going to be more traumatic. An escort was also employed to sit with the children and ensure that they were safely escorted into school. Robert's escort came to the door that morning but there was no way he was going to get into the taxi without a battle. Knowing my son as I do, I simply thought it best to pick him up and strap him in his seat. This I did, then kissed him goodbye and said, 'Mummy loves you, have a lovely day at school.'

I watched, desperate, as the taxi drove away, Robert was crying and waving to me. He looked so pitiful but I knew I had to let him go; he needed the help they could offer him. All this self-reassurance didn't stop the tears trickling down my cheeks.

My neighbour was also seeing her children off to school. She heard Robert's cries and watched as the taxi drove away. She asked me if I was OK! Then I broke down. I simply said, 'Not really.' Although I knew that Robert was getting the best help we could possibly hope for, this week was by far the most emotional one I can remember since his episode in the hospital.

As the days went by, Robert got used to the taxi and there was no more fuss going to school in the morning. In fact, after a few weeks he seemed a lot easier to direct and a lot happier on the mornings that he was going to school. He came home very tired each day though and there would often be tears and tantrums after school. I think it was fair to say that for the first half-term

Help!

(six weeks), Robert's behaviour actually took a turn for the worse. I had begun to think that things couldn't get any worse, but it was at this point that I too took a turn for the worse. I became very emotional and irritable. I was extremely low and totally exhausted, both physically and emotionally.

After the half-term break, which incidentally was a nightmare, Robert returned to school and I was invited to go in and chat about my concerns regarding his behaviour with the school nurse and Robert's teachers. This I did, and was again reassured that this was all actually quite normal behaviour; I had in fact been warned that things may get a little worse before starting to improve. This was all part of the settling in and I had quite simply forgotten that I should expect a certain degree of unsettling behaviour. This was, after all, such a big change for a child so young. I came away feeling that there was more of a reason to Robert's behavioural outbursts at that moment, and I resolved again to try and be a little more tolerant and understanding.

My patience improved once again, as did my confidence, thus enabling me to handle all situations better and be more patient with everybody.

After seeing the school nurse, I spent some time in the classroom with Robert and his teachers. I was delighted to be made so welcome. I was determined also that I was going to be involved with everything that happened to my children. I had a lovely time in the classroom with Robert, and it was great to be able to give him my undivided attention (Catherine was at home with Granddad). I was invited to go in and talk to the teachers whenever I felt the need and was made to feel that my presence was much appreciated (I had actually expected to feel like I was in the way).

So again my spirits were lifted and I felt more in control and able to cope. I was going to make sure that we did everything possible to make life good for our children, no matter what.

Robert had been at his new school for six weeks when he had his first full medical. I went to school with him that morning so as to be present at such an important time. I sat for a while with the school nurse and the medical officer, and we discussed Robert's history in some detail. We also talked about his present

Help!

problems: the learning disability, the developmental delay, and in particular the difficulties we were experiencing with Robert's social skills and general behaviour pattern. All of these I was reassured were *not* due to 'poor parenting', as seemed to have been the favoured statement of some doctors! After all, I had raised two very well-presented little girls, whose social graces had been remarked on frequently. Indeed, I had two compliments from professional acquaintances, both of whom said that the girls were a credit to us! What better compliment could a parent wish for? This is not to say that the girls didn't behave badly sometimes; it's just mostly they saved the 'off' moments for inside the safety and security of their own home, mostly for Mummy's attention.

As to the problems with Robert's behaviour, I felt greatly relieved that by now Robert was feeling more at ease in his new school and was starting to display some of his more negative behaviour in the classroom. Initially Robert came home with glowing reports of his behaviour through the day. I then began to think that perhaps he was only ever going to display symptoms at home and that his teachers would think I was imagining it all. I mentioned this on one occasion and thankfully was informed that most of the children were on their best behaviour initially and only when they had settled into the surroundings and had come to know and trust their teachers would they start to show signs of 'testing' behaviour.

The teachers had begun to notice some of Robert's more negative behaviour. They had also noted that, as I had always said, he found it very difficult to take adult direction, although that was improving slowly.

After we chatted for some time, Robert joined us and the medical officer examined him physically, this also being the first time anyone had taken a good look at him. Physically she had to agree that he was in pretty good shape. She did pass comments, however, on two points that I am still as yet a little baffled about. The first could probably be passed off as a familial trait. This point is that Robert's joints in his arms and legs tend to over-extend; he is very 'bendy'. As I said, this could be explained away quite simply and really isn't any big deal. The second point, which I remain a little concerned about, is that Robert has a very

Help!

hairy back; not unusual, you may think, but in fact he is fair-haired and yet has a great deal of dark hair particularly in the middle of his back following the line of his spine! The medical officer said that it may be nothing but she would mention it in her referral letter to the paediatrician. At last, the referral! I still found it hard to believe that at last someone had agreed that Robert should be assessed by a paediatrician. I began to feel that now Robert was in a special school, people were at least taking notice of his problems and trying to address them in a very positive way.

Robert had been undergoing a constant assessment period since starting at the special school, the results of which we were to discuss at a meeting with all the professionals involved with his care. At this meeting, we hoped that at last we might gain some insight into the cause of Robert's problems, and also more importantly we hoped to gain some idea as to what the future might hold for our son. It had already been suggested that Robert might not start at mainstream school in September when he was due to. I thought his teachers would probably recommend that he stayed where he was for the moment; after all, he had all the professionals to hand and much more attention which is certainly what he needed.

In the meantime, Robert would see the paediatrician at the local child development centre and have his hearing reassessed by the audiologist in school. Things seemed to be happening now for our son; people were beginning to respond with some very positive help.

Incidentally, at the end of the assessment, Robert had to perform the same tasks, as indeed he had for the health visitor, the clinical medical officer and the educational psychologist. I had by now watched Robert do these tasks four times. I was advised that he would be expected to repeat the exercise for the paediatrician. I knew the tests off by heart and I knew what Robert's response would be. It had been documented many times now in the written reports that had been sent to various professionals, and us, following each assessment. Who knows, maybe the fifth time around Robert would surprise us all and remember the tests and perform without hesitation; perhaps he'd score one hundred per cent!

Help!

Having said this, during the medical, for the first time I did notice some improvement in Robert's response to the assessment tasks. It was only very slight, but nevertheless it was an improvement.

People had told me that they could do wonderful things in just a short time at these schools. I must admit, though, I remained a little sceptical, especially after Robert's behaviour did deteriorate initially.

I will never forget, though, when the educational psychologist visited us at home, she told me a story about another family in a similar situation to ourselves. The child's father had refused to accept that there was any problem whatsoever; he was adamant that his child would not attend the special school. The mother, however, was distraught. She knew she needed help for her child so she sent him, against the father's wishes. It put an incredible strain on an already struggling relationship. It was, though, the father who three months later phoned the psychologist and thanked her for helping their son. The father said that he was like a different boy.

I had always remembered this and had secretly set a target. I had told myself by three months there would be some light at the end of the tunnel, that there would be some change in Robert and that life at home would become a little easier. I had to believe in something, to cling on to something to keep us going. As three months approached, I began to feel a little disappointed as I really couldn't see that anything had changed; certainly I could see no signs of improvement. As I said before, Robert's behaviour did actually deteriorate initially so I began to feel that we were really back to the point we had started at.

However, Robert had been in school for just over three months when we had the Easter break. I could now report that all of a sudden things were starting to change, for the better, I might add. I had started to notice little things that Robert had improved in. I had also noticed that life was a little easier at home with him. This could be due to many things. The baby, for a start, had become much more independent, and I had (I hope) become much more accepting of the situation and hopefully much more confident in my approach.

Help!

Much of the credit for the change must go to Robert himself as I'm sure he was trying very hard, but mostly the credit must go to the patience and effort put in by the staff at Robert's school. I have nothing but praise for them. Robert may never be a genius but he will have every chance to lead a normal life. He will at least be very well trained in his social and behavioural skills, which is where I had noticed most change.

Robert didn't exactly turn into a saint overnight but he was learning, albeit slowly. Robert's learning process and memory seemed to be very poor, and progress was very slow, but progress there was! I have always maintained that I am not the most patient person in the world. I have, however, tried very hard to be more patient and tolerant for the sake of my family.

If Robert were not to be recommended for mainstream school just then, of course we would be disappointed, but we would do whatever was best for our son and we would be guided by the professionals involved in his care.

To finish this chapter on a light note, Robert had taken part in his school production to celebrate Easter. Of course, I went in to see the performance. Unfortunately as Robert went onto the stage to take his place, he saw me! He then simply wanted to be with his mum. He was the one child on stage that all the mothers hoped would not be theirs. He cried and struggled, desperately trying to break free and come to me. His teacher hung on to him and carried on singing. Luckily there was lots of singing, so hopefully not too many people noticed!

I, too, desperately wanted to go to him! I was having to learn, though, to be stronger myself. I had begun to realise that by giving in to him all the time, I was actually doing him no favours. Robert had to learn to accept some discipline; he had to learn that he couldn't always have things exactly as he wanted. Sometimes, although it broke my heart, I simply had to be cruel to be kind. Robert had to learn to take his place in society as a decent, Christian person. I would be failing him miserably if I didn't try to teach him the realities of life. I couldn't wrap him up in cotton wool all the time, as I expect I had been guilty of doing in the past.

So, on this occasion, although I desperately wanted to go to

Help!

him, to make it all better, I knew that I mustn't. I would have undone all the good that the school had already done. So I imagined I had a bit of superglue on my seat and simply glued myself down. I'd never tried so hard to keep my bottom on such an uncomfortable seat!

Stop Trying to Be Perfect

Having read my book thus far, it may or may not surprise you, the readers, that while striving to deal with the trials and tribulations of raising a young family (and in particular with a child with special needs), I had also to contend with my own hidden problem. There is no better way to say this other than to just come out with it.

Unfortunately I have to be totally honest and admit that while trying too hard to achieve perfection, I had also become obsessive in almost everything I did. Apparently, though, I have now discovered that I am not alone in this. There are many sufferers affected in many different ways by this strange disease known as obsessive compulsive disorder (OCD). Perhaps many of you reading this will recognise similar patterns of behaviour in your own lives.

Obviously there are different degrees of severity in this condition and many ways that symptoms may manifest themselves. For me, the problem was associated with an overwhelming compulsion to clean and tidy practically everything. Some days were better than others; some days I could feel compelled to clean everything in sight over and over again, while other days were completely free of any abnormal compulsion. I am, however, one of the lucky ones. I recognised myself that I had a problem, and after having three children, I decided that enough was enough.

After many hours of soul-searching, I approached my GP and rather reluctantly explained the situation. I have to say that he was very understanding on this occasion, and extremely sympathetic. He was, in fact, the first to reassure me that I was not alone in this; he knew exactly what I meant and filled me with complete confidence that I was actually not going round the bend or anything like that. He also confirmed that I did not need to see a psychiatrist but suggested an appointment with a psychotherapist might be of some benefit.

Stop Trying to Be Perfect

I expect most people have to cope with some degree of stress at some time in their lives and that stress has many ways of presenting itself. Unfortunately this seemed to be my way of coping with stress. What a vicious circle, as this in itself produced yet more stress. Anyway, as I said, I am one of the lucky ones. I saw a wonderful lady who helped me to deal with the situation. My therapist very quickly established the root of the problem. If only I could have accepted it all so readily. I quite simply seemed to be trying too hard, trying to be the perfect mother, perfect wife and perfect home keeper. It seems ironic that all I want to do is be a good mother, yet in trying so hard I feel I have failed the children by wasting time on unnecessary activities.

Of course, I have here to sing the praises of counselling or therapy, whatever you like to call it, and would thoroughly recommend that anyone suffering with any type of problem should seek this kind of help before resorting to medicines or other costly treatments.

So, what happened next? What about Robert? Well, I wish I had something more definite to write here but I haven't. All I can say is I had to start accepting that we might never have any answers as to the cause of Robert's problems, or indeed what the future held for our son.

We finally saw the paediatrician with Robert but again I did not get the answers I was hoping for. I must admit that I did pin all my hopes on this meeting and had convinced myself that we would have something more concrete to go on by the end of this appointment. I had actually been advised not to expect too much from this meeting; this advice proved to be quite useful as I was a little more prepared for the disappointment than I thought I would be.

The doctor, however, did at least put us a little further down the road to the light at the end of the tunnel. He suggested that Robert should have some tests, the first time ever anyone had actually decided to do any proper physical testing in an attempt to discover any underlying factors that may be influencing Robert's development. He also warned me again not to get my hopes set on getting a diagnosis for Robert.

The doctor reassured me that there were many children in the

Stop Trying to Be Perfect

school like Robert, but likewise many of the parents had never discovered the reason for their child's problems. At the end of the day, these parents had to accept this and get on with life as best as they could. This situation I found particularly difficult as I like to know precisely where I stand and what is in store, so to speak. As it was, we had no idea whether Robert would catch up or 'recover' fully or whether he would always be 'a little behind'. I often wondered whether he'd be OK in perhaps one year, two years, five years or maybe never. Maybe Robert would never be 'normal' and would always require special assistance. Perhaps he'd always be dependent on us! I think what I am trying to say to parents here is that there has to come a point when, although the future looks daunting and is obviously a worry, one has to stop looking to the future and simply start enjoying the moment they are living in now. I have, I think, finally come to realise that we must accept Robert as he is now, love him as he is now and enjoy him as he is now.

In the meantime, Robert had his blood tests, which included a chromosome analysis and we were to wait as patiently as possible for the results. My husband and I also met the teachers at Robert's school to discuss the results of his assessment period in the early years unit. Shortly before this meeting, I received a written copy of the findings of the assessment. I was happy to read that the teachers had in fact come up with a pretty accurate description of our little boy and were in agreement with me on most areas of his progress and development. The report provided a focus for discussion at the meeting and was very useful as reference material, enabling us to work through Robert's problems systematically. It also helped me to remember the points I wanted to raise and specific concerns I had been meaning to discuss for some time. Robert's teachers were also concerned that I might be very disappointed if we couldn't discover a cause for his problems. They were very understanding and supportive. We discussed in detail the help Robert would get over the next year staying in the special school and some strategies we might try at home in order to relieve some of Robert's frustration.

The main problem highlighted was the frustration caused by some kind of delay Robert seemed to have interpreting the spoken word. When speaking to Robert, he seemed to take a long time to reply or respond to what had been said. You could see that he was trying to work out what had been said, but by the time he'd worked out how he wanted to reply, it came out back to front, in the wrong order and in a monotone. Sometimes, by the time he'd worked out what he wanted to say, he had actually forgotten the question or the answer, so he said nothing. His speech was also very loud with little expression in his voice. There seemed to be no variation in the tone of his voice. I was assured that Robert's hearing would be checked by the audiologist when he did a clinic at the school. I had been under the impression that all was well with Robert's ears once his grommets came out and was not anticipating any future problems in this area. However, at that time Robert's eardrum perforated, explaining a recent episode of quite severe regression in his behaviour!

It just so happened that Catherine was also poorly – on her first birthday, in fact! She had developed an infection and was rushed to hospital after suffering a febrile convulsion. Well, she had to be different, didn't she? This was one that we hadn't experienced before. I spent four days in the hospital with Catherine while the doctors tried to control her temperature and discover the source of the infection. This, incidentally, turned out to be a severe dose of tonsillitis! It was during this stay in hospital that I found I had a little more time on my hands than usual – one child instead of three! I took advantage of any naps Catherine had, and did the same myself. I did a lot of thinking while attending to her needs and realised that I had been quite guilty of neglecting the emotional needs of the girls. It is quite difficult while attending to the physical needs of one's children and the day-to-day management of the home to remember the truly important aspects of life, to ensure that the emotional and spiritual needs of each person in the family are also given sufficient consideration.

When presented with a child with special needs, it is difficult not to become so wrapped up in this one child's needs that one risks completely failing to meet the needs of the others. Perhaps I have been using the term 'special needs' too loosely; after all, as my own mother pointed out, are all children not special? Do they not all have special needs? I would, however, be hard pressed to find a kinder term to describe children such as Robert.

A few generations back, he would have been described by such harsh words as 'retarded' or 'backward' and he would probably have been hidden away from society. I am glad we are living now in a slightly more tolerant society. These children are at least acknowledged for what they are and given the special assistance they deserve. We have certainly been very fortunate in that Robert had the opportunity of extra help in a wonderful school and met some extremely caring and patient people there.

During Catherine's episode in hospital, I resolved to make more of an effort to ensure that all of our children were given more quality time together as a family and individually. I decided that it was time to be much more spontaneous and natural in my approach to raising the children and to try and run a more 'normal' household. The most noticeable change had to be in my attitude to Robert. I knew that I had to stop wrapping him up in cotton wool and defending him. Instead I had to treat him the same as I would treat the girls, especially with regard to discipline.

At about four years old, Robert reached a particularly delightful stage in his development. He became quite loving and loveable. At this stage we were not aware that he would later be diagnosed as autistic and this trait was actually quite unusual.

He was still, however, no angel; he remained extremely demanding and was prone to quite severe outbursts of temper. As most of this behaviour was due to the frustration caused by the delay Robert seemed to be experiencing interpreting the spoken word, Robert's teachers suggested backing up the spoken language with sign language. The teachers used Makaton sign language in the classroom and it had been noticed that he was much calmer in the classroom and seemed to respond much more readily to visual stimulus. I always said that we would try anything if we thought it would help Robert, so Mike and I learned the Makaton signs and tried to establish this in the home.

Robert was still very difficult to direct and negative in his behaviour. Simple tasks seemed to take him an eternity. It almost seemed that Robert felt that he just had to be as awkward as possible. The negative behaviour presented in the form of prolonged crying or temper tantrums. This behaviour seemed to go in cycles. We would have a couple of good weeks when there were few tantrums and Robert could be quite delightful and great to be with. This might then be followed by a bad phase when for weeks everything seemed to become a battle again and Robert's behaviour was extremely challenging. In these episodes, I would become quite low. During a good phase I kept telling myself not to be disappointed if a bad phase followed; however, during a particularly good phase or a long phase I always forgot and thought that this was it, he was really getting better. To this day this is true of Robert and I am often knocked back when a bad phase follows. This is hardly surprising as these phases can still be extremely exhausting. When one is constantly tired and emotional, it is difficult not to be irrational, irritable and very intolerant of everybody and everything!

The Parent and Child Game

When Robert was about five years old, and still at special school, he, Mike and I attended child and family therapy at the Osborn Clinic in Fareham. I have to sing the praises of the behavioural team as they engaged us in the 'Parent and Child Game', a wonderful approach to positive parenting (PP). I still use this approach today with the children now aged nineteen, seventeen and fourteen. Positive Parenting is a must for all parents. I can thoroughly recommend it and we will always be grateful to that team who will probably never know just how much they have helped us throughout the children's lives.

During one session of the Parent and Child Game, Robert and I were in the playroom with what on the inside of the room was a huge mirror but was actually a window. On the other side of the window sat the team observing Robert's behaviour and our interaction. The team would give me instructions in an earpiece to say positive statements to Robert and praise him for the good things he did. I was also told to ignore unwanted behaviour and not even make eye contact unless he was going to hurt himself or me.

On this occasion though, Robert had seen his dad leave the room and this time wanted Dad to play instead. He decided to try and get to Dad and spent half of the hour-long session trying to ram a push-along train through the door. I was told to look out of the window, chatting about what I could see. I talked about the cars and the trees, even about the people and what they were wearing. I was at no point allowed to look at Robert or speak to him until he came back into the room to play again. At this point I was allowed to praise Robert for coming back to play.

This session was particularly exhausting but with repetition over the months Robert started to respond to positive parenting and as I say, I still use this approach today. Thanks, team.

After the child and family therapy on the whole Robert did

seem to become calmer (although he still settled late in the evening and rose again at roughly 5.30 a.m.) This bit didn't help us as we were on the go from the moment he woke, and we still sometimes got very little rest.

As Robert's speech began to improve, he became quite a little chatterbox. Conversations could be held more easily with him and he could be a delight to listen to. His speech was still difficult to understand for strangers and we sometimes forgot this, as we were used to his pronunciation and his sentence order being incorrect.

Robert was still self-directed, making play with his sisters quite hair-raising at times. He tended to monopolise situations (and possessions, whether his or not) resulting in frequent clashes with high tempers and noise levels! Robert was making progress; he was improving and learning, albeit slowly. Many people commented on the changes in Robert after he started at the special school. I still have nothing but praise and admiration for the staff concerned.

The main thing I learnt from Robert's teachers at that time was to look for the good in everyone and home in on this. That is not to say that one has to ignore the bad, but it does make it easier to tolerate. There is good and bad in each and every one of us; none of us is perfect (no matter how hard we try) but we all have the potential to change for the better and it is this quality that must be nurtured and cultivated.

A child could not want for any more love than that bestowed on our three children. I may not always get it right but I will always try to do my best for the children, to raise them to be happy, healthy and loved.

Destination Diagnosis

At five and a half years old, Robert was finally seen by a child psychiatrist and diagnosed as having moderate learning difficulties, semantic/pragmatic language disorder with autistic tendencies and ADHD (attention deficit and hyperactivity disorder).

After struggling for such a long time, knowing ourselves that our son had quite a significant problem, the complete diagnosis was nonetheless quite a shock. We had not been as emotionally prepared for the final outcome as we had anticipated. We had, in fact, believed for some considerable time that no one in the medical profession was quite as prepared as ourselves to accept the severity of our son's condition.

I have to admit that my immediate reaction and feeling was actually relief! It was simply so reassuring to know that there was a reason for our son's strange behaviour. In that moment, when we left the doctor's office, I loved Robert more than ever before because I knew that he really couldn't help the way he was or the things that he did. He looked simply adorable again, just like my baby boy.

The calmness that followed Robert's diagnosis was also reflected in his behaviour. As my acceptance of the situation resulted in a more relaxed attitude, it also became more evident that Robert had become much calmer. I really could say that I had my baby back!

Unfortunately, the initial feelings of relief, acceptance and calm were soon overshadowed by such intense feelings of anger. I became angry at the whole world. So angry that this could have happened to us, to our son. I also began to ask why. No matter how hard I tried to search for the answers, I had to admit that none were forthcoming.

It would be dishonest of me if I were not to admit that the years of struggling with such a challenging child had begun to have a profound effect on those closest to Robert and their personal relationships. Although we felt that we had always accepted the situation as well as we could, we nevertheless continued to struggle with a rollercoaster of emotions. I, in particular, seemed to limp between ups and downs as no one could ever begin to imagine. I have taken great comfort in talking and writing about my experiences and have recently gained much encouragement from members of the Hampshire Autistic Society.

Despite the knowledge that we are far from alone in this situation, the greatest problem for me seems to be an intense feeling of isolation. Despite living in a house with four other people, I sometimes feel so alone and overwhelmed that at times it seems difficult to cope. I often wonder how other people cope, but they obviously do, as indeed we do. We have to! For the sake of our children, we somehow find the strength to carry on and do our best.

In continually striving to do our best and trying so hard, the constant struggle has taken its toll on family life. I am sorry to say that some friends and family alike seem to have rejected us in one way or another and failed to provide the comfort and support I would have expected. Maybe my expectations are far too high. I still maintain, as I always have, that at such times one discovers who one's true friends are. I am, however, happy to say that some of my closest friends have remained true and loyal, although they are few in number.

I wonder sometimes if the reason for the rejection is simply fear of the unknown. I can only say that we are afraid, too, and we still have no idea what the future holds for us or our son, but we will do our best to provide a happy life for all our children. No one can be expected to do any more.

I still feel hurt by this attitude, especially when it concerns one's own family but I am learning to live with it and have begun to see that it is actually the other person's problem and not my own.

If I were to be totally honest now, I would have to say that the biggest problem seemed to be the relationship between me and my husband. With little support and a constantly demanding young family, exhaustion seemed to have taken over and left little or no time for ourselves or each other. The other contributing factor seems to me to be the obvious stress and strain this kind of situation imposes on married life. The flood of emotions and seemingly endless number of problems appeared to have robbed us of any kind of normal life together. We both acknowledged that we had a lot of difficulties to overcome and resolved to try to overcome them and made a big commitment to each other to try to build a stronger relationship and to learn to compromise more in our marriage so that we could both provide a loving, secure and happy home life for Robert and his sisters.

So I think that what I am trying to say here is that in all people's lives there are lots of ups and downs but from my own experience there are more ups, and as long as there are more ups life is good and fun and full of surprises and enjoyment at every turn.

For Robert, at six years old, life was good. His hyperactivity and learning difficulties were his main problem but he was unaware that he was different from anybody else. He had not questioned why he went to a different school, and until such time as he did then we remained happy that, in that instance, the age-old saying of 'ignorance is bliss' certainly remained true. That is not to say that Robert was or is ignorant! Far from it. Underneath it is obvious that there is a wealth of intelligence waiting to be unlocked.

A New Beginning

Tonight, 10 September 2006, after a very moving and emotional scene in *Eastenders*, I have felt compelled to write again after a break of ten years. Those ten years were filled with many highs and lows, with happiness and with sadness.

The scene in *Eastenders* in which Billy and Honey discover that their beautiful newborn baby girl has Down's syndrome shows them devastated, but there are more emotional scenes to follow. During the following scenes, they discuss how and when, or even if, to tell the family.

Unlike Billy and Honey, for us there was never any one day that we realised Robert was so special; it was a sort of slow realisation over his early years. There was never any disappointment or upset relating to Robert's problems, we just thought he was 'special'!

Obviously there were trying times to follow but I believe that God sent Robert to us for a special reason yet to be discovered.

The earlier chapters in this book describe life in the 1990s, trying to raise a young family with a child who has special needs. Originally the book was to be called *Bless Our Children* and the earlier chapters are highly emotional and span the first six years of our son's life.

Robert, diagnosed with a moderate learning disability, autism and attention deficit and hyperactivity disorder (ADHD), is now a teenager and life is still very unpredictable.

In the last ten years, I myself have been too ill to write after being diagnosed with severe postnatal depression with obsessive compulsive disorder (OCD) after the birth of our third child, Catherine.

Having come so far after being so ill, I now feel ready to continue the story of life in the twenty-first century with a teenager who has such complex needs.

Perhaps I should continue where I left Chapter Twelve, with Robert in special needs school in Fareham.

A New Beginning

At the time, we were living in Park Gate with our three young children. A house move to Waterlooville was suggested to be near family and friends who could offer support. The move proved to be particularly distressing due to the family difficulties, as my husband refused to move. I was particularly low at the time, so against all my better judgement I proceeded to move myself and the children without my husband to our new area, Waterlooville.

Our oldest daughter Jennifer was just seven years old and I had managed to secure a place for her at the local Catholic primary school, St Peter's, in Waterlooville. Robert was to remain in special needs school in Fareham and transport was arranged to keep him there until such time as a change of school would be appropriate. Catherine, our youngest daughter, was enrolled in a local nursery school.

After a few months, my husband and I decided to make a go of it again and we managed to buy a larger, older house in Purbrook. We thought that all the extra space would be great for the children but the house needed to be completely refurbished. Funds were low after the move so we had to redecorate a room at a time when money allowed.

I think the shabby surroundings in which we were living was the penultimate catalyst in provoking my own illness. The final straw was when our youngest daughter Catherine needed the same tonsils, adenoids and grommets surgery which we had already experienced to such detriment with first Robert and then Jennifer.

I was already pretty ill when Catherine was admitted for her operation at three years old. I managed to hold it all together while she was in hospital and at home recovering. However, just one week after her op, I was admitted to St James' Hospital in Portsmouth as I was unable to care for myself let alone the children.

This was to be a particularly distressing time, as I was to spend a large part of the next two years in this hospital. I missed many special events in the children's lives and I now feel guilty about this because I feel the time away from the children should have been a time for me to be able to control my mental illness. I felt that I was robbed of these very special moments in the children's

A New Beginning

lives, which could never be replaced. However, it was my love for the children and their love for me that gave me the determination to get better and now we have many special moments.

The two events that I missed which meant the most to me were Jennifer's First Holy Communion and Robert's transfer to mainstream school to be with his sisters and cousins.

I didn't actually miss Jennifer's First Holy Communion, because although I was in hospital at the time, I was given home leave to be with Jennifer at the service and afterwards for a party at home. Although I felt like I was there in body, which was so special for Jennifer, I knew deep down I wasn't there in mind and the memory of this event remains a bit of a blur. However, I have the most beautiful photos to remind me and everyone was so pleased to see me there.

Robert's transfer to mainstream school to be with his sister was much more harrowing for me. At the time I had been admitted to the Marchwood Priory Hospital in Southampton as an emergency patient as there were no beds in Portsmouth for me. I cried that day because I felt that, as I was there for his first day in special school, this was of far greater importance as I knew it would be so challenging for Robert. I cried and cried as I told the nurse that I had let him down so badly as he really needed his mum that day.

Robert's transfer to the new school at the end of the infants actually went very successfully.

I called this chapter 'A New Beginning' because it marked several new beginnings for the family. The first is that I myself have been able to continue writing Robert's story after two years' severe mental illness and eight years' recovery and also it was a new beginning for the family in Waterlooville and for the children in their new school.

No More Drugs

After the move to Waterlooville, Robert was transferred to the local paediatrician and the local child and adolescent psychiatrist.

At the age of six Robert was (finally) rediagnosed as having a moderate learning disability, autism and ADHD. The letter of diagnosis was actually sent to Robert's new headmistress (Mrs Renault). Thankfully she saw fit to send us a copy of the letter.

At that time, Robert's behaviour was so unpredictable and inappropriate and he found it difficult to concentrate so the doctor prescribed a drug called Ritalin to help him.

When Robert started on the Ritalin, he had just moved into the juniors at school. He was to have three tablets a day, which meant his teachers had to give him a tablet at school. It very quickly became apparent that Ritalin was not the drug for Robert. We had agreed to the trial as we really believed it would help him especially with his concentration and school work. Ritalin had such a detrimental effect so that we soon decided that drugs were not the answer for Robert. His teachers were particularly pleased when we took him off it as on the drug he had been so unresponsive he was like a zombie! We vowed then that psychiatric drugs were not the solution for Robert. After this, his teachers reported that he was responding much better and they actually reported that he had even started to show signs of a cheeky little sense of humour. As a matter of fact he has a wonderful personality. He is very sensitive and caring, yet sometimes extremely negative and difficult to direct.

After the transition to St Peter's Catholic primary school in Waterlooville, Robert seemed to progress fairly well and was reasonably settled but he was never as happy as he was at Heathfield Special School in Fareham. There were incidents that need to be mentioned and discussions that should be reported.

As Robert already had a statement of special educational

needs, we were to be invited in to school once a year for his statement review. We would discuss his progress so far and aims for the coming year.

Robert's favourite teacher, Mrs Whitfield, was very honest when we met for the first time; I can remember her words as though it were yesterday.

She said, 'Mrs Austin, I'll be honest: I've never taught a child like Robert but I promise I will do my best for him!'

And she did! She taught Robert for two years in the juniors, Year Three and Year Five and they were Robert's happiest times in mainstream school. At the end of Year Five, Robert begged me to let him stay in Year Five with Mrs Whitfield for ever.

Year Four with Mrs Crawford was also successful. She did her utmost to try and understand Robert's needs and to accommodate him in the mainstream setting.

I have also to mention Robert's helpers, for Years Three and Four, Mrs Guest, and Years Five and Six, Mrs Cairns. Both these ladies seemed to have an inexhaustible wealth of patience so I must thank them for their efforts.

Meeting Dan

One thing that stands out in my memory of Robert's time in the junior school is that he only ever had one friend, Danny, another boy with special needs who has remained Robert's only friend throughout the junior and senior school. Danny was also later diagnosed as autistic, in the senior school. Initially most of the relationship was one-sided. As Robert was new to the school, Danny took him under his wing and tried to help him but he was a lot more verbal, confident and physical than Robert. Danny would unintentionally push Robert in the right direction in an attempt to help. Robert couldn't handle this in the early days as he disliked being touched by anyone except his parents. Over the years, Robert and Danny have come to some kind of non-verbal understanding and Robert can now tolerate Danny much better. They remained good friends even though they were in different classes in the seniors.

The two boys were completely different in character as Danny has active autism whereas Robert is more passive. I hope they will remain friends for ever.

Another event that sticks in my mind and is of particular importance was the day the school tried to take Robert on a walk from school to the local shops. This was of significance because Robert was also diagnosed with hypermobility in his joints, which for Robert means that it is difficult and painful for him to walk or run very long distances. He also has a rather unusual gait, which makes walking very tiring.

This diagnosis was never referred to in writing but I recall several times verbally informing Robert's teachers that he could not walk far, so I was disappointed that this should have occurred.

What actually happened is that after walking all the way from school to Waterlooville town centre, probably a distance of one and a half miles, Robert sat down on the pavement and refused to walk back. Robert was unable to verbalise that his legs were

Meeting Dan

actually hurting and his behaviour was reported as being 'difficult'! Because it took longer than expected to get back to school, after Robert's apparent 'refusal' to co-operate, he actually missed an important transition afternoon at the senior school he was to attend. The senior school were not informed of this incident and were consequently waiting for quite some time for Robert to arrive.

Robert was actually so distressed after this event that a further situation arose the following morning when we arrived in the school car park to begin the school day. On this occasion Robert refused to get out of the car to go into school. I tried my best to encourage him to get out of the car but I soon realised that unless I physically removed him from the car he wasn't going to budge! I wasn't prepared to use physical force as it would be both difficult for me to do and very undignified and unfair on Robert. I finally decided to send Robert's sisters into the school office to explain the situation in order to get help. I expected that the headmistress or Robert's teacher would come to our aid but in fact his teaching assistant came to the car to see what she could do. I'm not sure if the school had ever come across such a situation, but after more verbal attempts to encourage Robert to get out of the car to no avail, it was suggested that I take Robert home for a 'sickie'!

I was somewhat bemused, as I thought that this was sending the wrong message to Robert as I could imagine a repetition of this situation the next time Robert was unhappy about going into school.

I think the point I'm trying to make here is the importance of communication between parents and school staff and also among the staff in general.

The Transition to Oaklands

When it came time to move school, the junior school and the senior school initiated a period of transition, during which time Robert was to spend several afternoons in the senior school in order to familiarise himself with his new surroundings. The junior school also arranged a social story, which included pictures and writing, to describe Robert's new school and demonstrate what he would be doing there. This was very useful and the inevitable change from juniors to seniors actually went quite well.

Robert's first year in Year Seven at Oaklands was relatively uneventful. He seemed to settle quite well but he was never really very happy; he didn't smile so much and he certainly didn't laugh much.

I had anticipated a certain amount of regression as this often happened after significant changes in Robert's circumstances. I never really thought that he would cope with school life in a mainstream secondary school with 1,400 students. Even though the school had a special needs team with a special educational needs co-ordinator, I knew it would be an extremely challenging period in Robert's life. Robert was to continue to be reviewed yearly and at his first statement review in the seniors we were reassured that Robert was, despite my reservations, doing very well!

The thing that stands in my memory most about Year Seven was that Robert had two seizures. These started while Robert was in Year Six during transition time. I'm not sure if you would really call them seizures but I can't think of another way to describe what was happening to Robert. He would just literally collapse and be unconscious for anywhere between five minutes and an hour and a half at his worst. He didn't shake; he was just out cold. When he eventually came round he would be unresponsive and floppy. On two of these occasions, Robert actually went blue around the lips and paramedics were called as he

The Transition to Oaklands

needed oxygen therapy. On both these occasions he was taken to casualty but tests revealed nothing. Later on an EEG was to show that epilepsy was not the cause of these very alarming episodes.

We eventually learnt to cope with these episodes but it was extremely frightening as we didn't know when, or even if, Robert was going to come around.

After a year or two, these events settled down to approximately one every six months. We learnt to adapt and luckily, because I was not working, I could at least drop everything to be with Robert at these very difficult times.

Robert's second year in the seniors, Year Eight, was relatively uneventful except to say that, despite being assured that Robert was 'doing fine', I became more and more concerned as Robert became even less happy and more and more negative, difficult, obstinate and frequently verbally abusive.

Parents' evenings in Years Seven and Eight were very encouraging and many positive comments were forthcoming but I remained concerned as a couple of teachers suggested that Robert was or might be in the wrong environment!

I had secretly thought for some time that Robert would be much happier in a smaller, quieter and calmer establishment. I voiced my concerns at Robert's statement review. I was once again reassured that Robert was actually coping really well; indeed, his form tutor suggested that removing Robert from Oaklands at this time would be quite catastrophic as he was by now beginning to 'come out of himself'!

For the second time, I was convinced that leaving Robert in Oaklands was for the best.

Year Nine parents' evening was particularly distressing for me as, after being told repeatedly that Robert was coping really well and doing fine, I actually began to think that despite Robert's diagnosis, maybe I was imagining everything that was wrong with him and had even convinced myself that maybe he would be able to cope with the average ten GCSEs!

At the start of Year Nine parents' evening, I really thought that Robert would be able to sit all subjects to GCSE, but as the evening went on and we saw each of Robert's subject tutors, the list of possible subjects that Robert would actually be sitting

The Transition to Oaklands

became fewer and fewer until by the end of the session it was revealed that Robert was only considered capable of sitting four subjects to GCSE. I was horrified, not with Robert but with the school, because they had led me to believe that he was doing much better than this. Once again, as the reality unveiled itself, I became very disappointed with the school and the state education system.

As Robert had a statement of special educational needs but was in a mainstream school, he was obliged to sit the minimum core subjects, namely maths, English and science, to GCSE exam. This is even more ironic because English is Robert's worst subject. At fourteen years old, Robert was still not using punctuation or spelling well, yet he was expected to do the two English exams, that is, language and literature, both pet hates of Robert.

To add to this frustration, Robert was expected to choose an 'option' from a list of extras, which apparently he had to do, also to exam level. After exhausting nearly all of the options because teachers advised that he was not capable of taking their subject at exam level, he was left with cookery as the only option. Robert himself didn't want to do any of the options, especially cookery, because although he loved cooking, he had previously been warned that the cookery GCSE involved sixty per cent of the mark going to written coursework, and Robert hated writing! Being left with no alternative, we had to sign him up for cookery, even though his tutor had already advised that he was not a suitable candidate!

We were, however, informed that it was 'necessary' for him to do another subject. I'm not sure if there is any legislation about the required number of exams to be taken by a child with SEN in a mainstream school. I must ask next time we meet at school.

At the same time, there was better news for Robert as he had been accepted to do a school/college link, one day a week at the local South Downs College. Coincidently, Robert would be studying cookery which he loved, but in a course where practical work was of greater importance. We were all relieved about this and Robert adapted well to one day a week in the college's catering department. South Downs College has its own special needs team and the whole college experience has been a much

The Transition to Oaklands

more positive one for Robert, coming at a time when Robert probably encountered the most difficult time so far in his life, namely adolescence!

The Beginning of the Depression

Apart from college once a week to cheer him up, Robert found Year Ten, age fourteen, probably the most distressing time in his life. Robert's self-esteem was already very low with the whole senior school experience and then I can only assume that at fourteen years old, he hit adolescence, a thoroughly distressing and traumatic time for any teenager but for Robert it really knocked him off balance. I began to refer to Robert as my 'AA Man' (Autistic Adolescent). It seemed a kinder way of describing a young man with so many difficulties.

At this time in Robert's young life, I have to say that he was at his most difficult, even more so than as a frustrated toddler with no speech. I believed that Robert needed then more patience, tolerance and support than ever before, but once again I was accused of overindulging him by family and friends, which I found particularly upsetting as I too needed patience and support! Those who remarked most knew exactly about Robert's earlier life and his diagnosis. This was really hurtful, but I remained determined that I would always be there for Robert, particularly when what was needed most was a reassuring hug from Mum. And if a mother can't give a hug to reassure her own son, then who can? I will hug Robert until the end of my days if that's how he seeks reassurance. At this time more than ever, we had to demonstrate to Robert that he was indeed a loved and worthwhile person.

In Robert's fifteenth year, he regressed so much that his behaviour became more unpredictable and inappropriate than ever. He was extremely negative and difficult to direct, as he had been as a young boy. Now that he was becoming a young man, I think he became so confused about the things that were happening to his mind and body that he could not cope with himself, let alone anybody else. He became verbally abusive and withdrew to the sanctuary of his own room and his Playstation, where I think

The Beginning of the Depression

he felt safe. He refused to join in family occasions and withdrew into himself so much that, with his already low self-esteem, he was in fact seen by the child psychiatrist who described him as being so vulnerable that he was very near the point of clinical depression. I was even more horrified when she suggested that if he did not improve we might like to try him on an antidepressant drug called Prozac!

Having had a very negative history myself with psychiatric drugs, I was determined that there was no way my fourteen-year-old son was going to be put on drugs. I vowed that my husband and I would help him overcome his depression naturally. We tried really hard to wean Robert off his Playstation and computer games. I tried taking all the children outdoors more, particularly in the evening with the spring and summer dawning. We encouraged more outside activities like his trampoline, which he loves, and table tennis and even got in a six-foot snooker table for the garage. We had to be more tolerant and particularly more encouraging than we ever had been before. Thankfully, Robert managed to shrug off the depression naturally, with love and support from those nearest to him and most definitely without psychiatric drugs.

With all this going on, I tried one more desperate time to remove Robert from the anxiety of a busy modern secondary school with the hustle and bustle of 1,400 students. I found a school within Hampshire Autistic Society where there were only ten students and where Robert would be able to benefit from the various specialists who would be supporting him.

I approached Hampshire Education Authority for funding and even secured the support of all Robert's doctors and specialists, and, I believe, his tutors. I also managed to get written support from our local MP the Right Honourable Sir Michael Mates, and our local councillor.

I felt encouraged as over the last six months I had really begun to think that nobody cared and there was little or no hope for Robert and his future. That's when I thought of calling this book *Too Late for Robert*, as I began to think that I had left it too late to get expert help for him.

Hampshire Education Authority finally agreed to do a further statutory assessment of Robert's special educational needs, a sort of 'new' statement to see if Robert's needs had changed significantly enough to require a change of educational establishment this late in Robert's school career.

At about this time, Robert's teachers took him on a day trip to Dorset. While standing on the cliffs, Robert was heard to say that one day he would come back and throw himself off Old Harry Rocks to kill himself. I realised then that at this stage in Robert's life he was an extremely vulnerable young man and I knew I had to do something to help him.

In January 2007, at the Year Ten parents' evening, Robert became so distressed that he walked out of the meeting. When I found him, he was crying and begging to go home. The assistant head teacher saw Robert in this state and said, 'We need to design a package of education appropriate for Robert's needs!' Over the next six months, this did not happen.

I don't feel that the school is entirely responsible for letting Robert and our family down, but feel very strongly that schools are being guided by the government who seem to be closing as many special schools as possible and trying to integrate as many children with special needs into mainstream schools. If this policy is to be successful, then the government surely needs to supply funding for all those schools to employ expertise in every area of disability. I believe that this is neither practical nor possible. While I believe wholeheartedly in inclusion for all peoples, there will always be a need for special schools. Not every child with a disability can be integrated successfully into mainstream school. These children are, after all, so very special, they will always need special people to help them.

Turnaround

The draft of Robert's new statement did not arrive until after the children had all broken up from school for the summer holidays. Robert had only one year to remain in the seniors and was then unsure of what he would like to do when he left school at the age of sixteen.

Having visited Aspin House in Southampton, which is one of Hampshire Autistic Society's educational centres, we were convinced that even though it would mean weekly boarding, with only ten students and all the expert care, Robert would benefit much more from such an establishment. I think that Hampshire Education Authority were probably very near to agreeing and providing the funding for such a placement based on the medical evidence provided by Robert's specialists.

After the summer break we were hoping that Robert might be about to begin a new era at Aspin House, but with the September term approaching and after all the efforts to help Robert recover, he was so much better that one day he said to me, 'Mum, I think I'd like to go back to Oaklands and try to do my four GCSEs!'

We were so shocked and at the same time relieved so we agreed that Robert had made his decision and that we would support him through this, even though many people had eventually fought on Robert's behalf to remove him from mainstream school.

To all those people who wrote letters of support on Robert's behalf, please don't feel that your time was wasted, because if he hadn't recovered so well, then he certainly would have needed to be removed from Oaklands. All I can say is that we will always be eternally grateful for that support and are now just only too pleased that it has all turned out well for Robert.

Although initially we had hoped Robert would go to Aspin House, as he would have all the expertise and experience of professional people extremely well prepared to care for youngsters with autism, secretly the thought of sending him to even a weekly boarding school was breaking my heart, but I felt I had to do what was best for Robert and not myself. I was also terrified that, especially at night, Robert would be alone without Mum to turn to if he needed reassurance.

I am more than glad that, as it turned out, Robert chose to stay with the family at home and at Oaklands and it proved that expertise is not always the answer. In fact, thankfully it turned out that what Robert needed most was the good old-fashioned love, patience and support of his family.

Incidentally you may all be pleased to know that Robert was offered a place at catering college at South Downs to start in September 2008, after a very successful interview with the head chefs, to whom I have to thank a lot for restoring my faith in human kindness. Andy and Paul made Robert feel completely at ease during his interview and Robert actually smiled all the way through the meeting. I had to mention it as he hadn't smiled like that in a long time. They also reassured me that Robert would be extremely well supported by a massive dedicated team of support workers led by the special needs leader Bee, whom Robert had already met.

With his love of cooking back on track, I really do believe that at last Robert has something to look forward to and I am much more hopeful for his future.

I think Robert will have a much more positive experience at college. It's such a shame that his memories of senior school and the whole 'Oaklands thing', as he calls it, are of an extremely negative and overwhelming time. If you ask Robert now what he thinks of school, he would probably, as is usual, say 'poo'! That is not to say that Oaklands is not a good school; indeed my girls have had a great time there! So much so that Jennifer didn't want to leave so she stayed on at Oaklands sixth-form college after gaining five A-grade passes, one of which was an A*, and five B-grade passes at GCSE. I have to sing her praises here as she hopes to do seven years at university to get a PhD and become a doctor of archaeology.

What I think I am trying to say here is that while Oaklands, like most other mainstream schools, is brilliant for our academic students, schools such as these are not yet prepared to receive children with such difficult and diverse special educational needs.

Robert's Greatest Day

To finish on a good note, we have had Year Eleven (GCSE year) parents' evening. Despite predictions of low grades at his four exams, I remain extremely proud that Robert even attempted GCSEs. To add to this, in his final school term, for the first time in all his school years, Robert has actually read out loud in front of his whole class in not only one but in two subjects, namely English and RE! What an achievement! I am so proud of Robert. He has been so brave.

After his depression earlier in the year, Robert has achieved a complete turnaround. I am proud to say that now Robert is turning into an extremely thoughtful and polite young man.

I hope that this in some way reflects his Catholic education, but mostly I would like to think that this reflects the manner in which we, his parents, have tried to raise him.

I would like to think that we have taught all three of our children, from a very young age, with or without special needs, to be polite and respectful and to be decent, Christian people.

Bearing this in mind, I would like to include at this point a poem that Robert himself wrote for a piece of RE homework about marriage. Robert never actually handed this homework in (his memory, eh?) and I found it recently in a bottom drawer. I have now submitted this to his RE teacher for marking. I would like to think that this poem, as I believe it comes from the heart, will gain Robert a very respectable grade. Robert's poem is also hopefully to be included in HAS (Hampshire Autistic Society) monthly magazine.

Robert's Poem

Marriage is about sharing all the joys of life
With love so special between man and wife.
Living together, alongside each other,

Robert's Greatest Day

> Helping one another, with a bond so tight
> That can't be broken. Living all their lives together,
> Loving and cherishing one another.
> You are so special, you are the love of my life.
> You're the soul that guides me,
> Holding me up and supporting me,
> The stars are your eyes, the sunset is your beauty
> And my love for you is eternal.
> You're always there beside me
> Helping me through my life.
> My thoughts are always yours, to hold in your heart.
> While I dream I think of you,
> You set my life alight!

I would like to think that we have taught Robert and his sisters to love themselves and accept themselves as worthwhile, unique and loveable people and that as they go through their lives they in turn will be able to radiate most importantly love and laughter to all with whom they come into contact!

Robert has been an extremely brave young man through his education, particularly in the fact that he has managed to cope with the mainstream school system and I hope that he lights the way for others who may follow him in the government's inclusions policy. I would like to think that, through our communications with the whole school team, things will improve for other youngsters with special needs who have to cope with the very daunting and overwhelming experience of mainstream education.

Here would be a good point to thank Mrs Cozens, Robert's head of year for Years Ten and Eleven, who has been the most supportive of both Robert and the family, especially for me as I have also found this whole experience particularly distressing.

I'm sure you can agree that, like most mums, I have only tried to get the best for my children. Quite remarkably, Robert coped extremely well with the GCSE weeks. He attended every exam, tried his best to answer questions, wrote well and even got himself home alone (never before attempted) as I was poorly. He remained happy and positive and, no matter what grades he gets, I believe he deserves a medal just for trying!

Robert's Greatest Day

Robert has much to look forward to at catering college with Chef Paul at his side, with whom he seems to have a wonderful relationship, built upon mutual respect and understanding. We wish him every success in this and we, his parents and sisters, are the proudest of all because Robert is our special boy.

I think that all that remains to be said is that, no matter what qualification or what level of independent living Robert may achieve (even if he chooses to always live at home with Mum and Dad), we will always remain extremely proud and always be there to support and reassure him.

The most important thing is that, no matter what Robert does or where he is, I just always want him to be happy.

Robert and Dan have been warmly welcomed to join a group of young adults on a pilgrimage to Lourdes this summer. The group is a church-led youth group called SAYIT from Southampton and the youngsters range in age from fourteen- to twenty-five-year-olds.

Although the group is not made up of youngsters with special needs, Robert and Dan have been made to feel most included and I believe this really marks the integration of youngsters with disabilities into groups of more able youngsters.

I would love to think that Robert and Dan light the way for those people in our community who deserve to be recognised wholeheartedly for the unique, individual and wonderful people they are.

There will, of course, always be youngsters so severely affected by their circumstances that total inclusion may never be possible. I believe we must stand up for our special schools, which will always be much needed and in particular for the very special people who work in these wonderful environments and will always be much appreciated by our families.

God bless you and good luck, boys. Have fun!

Epilogue – Robert's Miracle

Robert and Dan returned from Lourdes with the most wonderful tales to tell. It had been an extremely successful trip and, although neither boy went with any religious intention, I do believe that a little bit of a miracle may have occurred for my Robert! I didn't send Robert to Lourdes hoping for a cure because I actually didn't want to change Robert; we love him just the way he is. I did, however, think that the trip would be fantastic for him socially and would be beneficial to his independence. However, I also secretly hoped that, as I hold strong religious beliefs and now use my skills and faith to help instruct at church meetings, there may be some influence to help get Robert back to the faith, because while I occasionally encourage my children and remain hopeful, I would never force their involvement at this age.

Robert has, in fact, returned to church once since Lourdes but that was more of a gentlemanly thing to do as he was escorting me following surgery when I couldn't go unaided. In fact, though, Robert's miracle was more subtle and other people wouldn't even notice. You see, Robert never cuddled anybody, other than me, once past the baby years. However, on his return from Lourdes, Robert actually hugged everybody in his group when they said farewell. He also exchanged phone numbers and email addresses with the promise of keeping in touch, something he'd never done before. In fact, Robert had only actually been brave enough to start using a phone at all in this last year. As if this weren't enough, Robert also came home, went straight upstairs into his big sister's room and said, 'Hug, Jenny.' They hugged and Jennifer was reduced to tears, another rarity. I said to her afterwards that it must have been worth sixteen years to wait for that hug because it was worth it for me to see it!

Robert has also excelled himself in his GCSEs and achieved far better results than teachers and computers could ever have predicted for him. Robert was originally entered for four GCSEs

Epilogue – Robert's Miracle

and predicted four grade Es if he worked to the very best of his ability. I suspected that even this might be difficult as, in the past, the exam experience had been so traumatic that he had managed only to write his name and then panicked when he read the questions and, being unable to comprehend or think what to write, he wrote nothing and was actually ungraded.

As I said in the last chapter, Robert did so well in the last six months of school that he was entered for a further two GCSEs at the last minute. He was actually asked first if he'd like to try for these exams. Incidentally one of these was RE, which, although he said he found boring, he was responding well to. Robert agreed to do these exams and his teacher said it showed a very mature approach to his education, even if it was late in the day.

Robert was so nervous on results day that he actually returned to the car, where he'd asked me to stay while he went to get them, with the envelope unopened. When I asked him why, he just said, 'Oh, maybe I'll open it later!' I guessed he might be a bit worried so I offered to look first if it would make him feel better. He agreed and I opened the envelope. At the last moment I had an inkling that Robert had, in fact, pulled out all the stops for these exams and was quite hopeful for maybe even a D but I didn't want either of us to be disappointed so I said nothing. Imagine my surprise when the first result I saw was the RE grade and, against all odds, through another miracle or actually more of Robert's hard work, he scored a C! This was probably when I realised that all the heartache of Robert's earlier difficult years, and all the hard work, patience and tolerance had paid off. As far as I was concerned, that day, Robert's results were as much of an achievement as all the A★s achieved by the A-grade students who had been predicted them. To me, that day, Robert was the Superstar!

Robert left Oaklands with three grade Es, two grade Ds and a fantastic grade C in probably one of the most difficult, controversial, thought-provoking but sincere subjects, which I'm sure any employer would think shows great strength of character.

So to add to Robert's wonderful sense of humour, with which he entertains and inspires me continuously, he also now seems to have acquired great strength of character and determination.

Robert is training to be a chef now, doing extremely well and

Epilogue – Robert's Miracle

enjoying himself, which is most important. He is loyal to his special friends and loving and supportive to me and his sisters and some close family members.

I wish I could say at this point that everything was as good and positive as the previous paragraphs but, unfortunately not all in life is a bed of roses. The children cannot always be protected from the harsh lessons life sometimes throws up but I like to think that, with openness and honesty and my undying support, I can at least help them to realise that we can turn most of life's experiences into something positive. Life is a constant learning curve and our experience of that moulds and shapes our personalities and our outlook.

Unfortunately, the only bad thing to happen lately happened to be a hugely life-changing experience for Robert and his sisters as, I am genuinely sorry to say, their daddy and I were unable to remain together in our support for the children.

The children and I are now living in a new little house with lovely neighbours and surroundings and have made a completely fresh start, a new start, a new beginning, and we have lots to look forward to. Robert and his sisters still have their moments. Teenagers, you know! I can only hope now that they will be as happy as I am in our new home and happy in their lives, wherever they are and whatever they end up doing. I love you, guys!

I will remain determined to be a good mother and to set a good example to the children and to ensure that the profession of full-time devoted motherhood is recognised as a worthwhile, significant and important role in society.

Printed in Great Britain by
Amazon.co.uk, Ltd.,
Marston Gate.